The
Lost Villages
of England

The Lost Villages of England

Leigh Driver • *Photography by* Stephen Whitehorne

NEW HOLLAND

This edition published in 2008 by New Holland Publishers (UK) Ltd
London • Cape Town • Sydney • Auckland

www.newhollandpublishers.com

Garfield House, 86–88 Edgware Road, London, W2 2EA, UK

80 McKenzie Street, Cape Town 8001, South Africa

Unit 1, 66 Gibbes Street, Chatswood, NSW 2067, Australia

218 Lake Road, Northcote, Auckland, New Zealand

ISBN 978 1 84773 218 7

Publishing Manager: Jo Hemmings
Senior Editor: Steffanie Brown
Designer: Alan Marshall
Cartographer: Bill Smuts
Production: Joan Woodroffe

Reproduction by Pica Digital Pte Ltd, Singapore
Printed and bound by Kyodo Printing Co Pte Ltd, Singapore

COVER AND PRELIMINARY PAGES

FRONT COVER: The old manor house at Hampton Gay, Oxfordshire

SPINE: A crumbling church tower at Godwick, Norfolk.

BACK COVER: The lofty tower of the old church at Covehithe, Suffolk (left); Hawthorne
scrub reclaiming Hound Tor, Dartmoor (Devon) (middle); The old Rectory at Tyneham,
Dorset (right)

OPPOSITE: The 13th-century mansion that still stands at Stokesay, Shropshire

HALF-TITLE PAGE: Old house crumbling into the sea at Hallsands, Devon

TITLE SPREAD: A view of the old church from its graveyard at Segenhoe, Bedfordshire

PAGES 6–7 (left to right): Stone foundations of Hundatora, now known as Houndtor; an old
fireplace is still visible amidst the ruins of a former home in Tyneham, Dorset; the shell of the
old church at Covehithe, Suffolk; a crumbled cottage at Greenhow Hill, Yorkshire

CONTENTS

PREFACE

In his introduction to the 1998 reissue of *The Lost Villages of England*, by economic historian Professor Maurice Beresford, Professor Christopher Dyer comments that it is 'one of those rare books that changed an academic subject, or rather invented a new subject for investigation and debate'. It is thus with great humility that we have borrowed the title of Professor Beresford's seminal work on the nature, identification and study of England's deserted settlements, acknowledging the enormous debt owed to the man who, alongside Professor W. G. Hoskins and Mr J. G. Hurst, blazed trails across the English landscape for us to follow.

I have not attempted an update of Professor Beresford's work, the need for which he himself said had been obviated by the publication in 1971 of the book *Deserted Medieval Villages* (a selection of studies co-edited by Beresford and Hurst). Rather, this book is a personal odyssey, inspired by the work of Beresford, Hoskins, Hurst and later Richard Muir (author of *The Lost Villages of Britain*, 1985). It was written as the result my own journey around England, during which I visited the wonderfully evocative sites of many vanished rural communities. Of the 3,000 or more known deserted settlements this country has to offer, just 57 have been chosen. Hopefully, they will be considered a representative selection of the best sites in England today, and may perhaps inspire readers to set off on journeys of discovery themselves. I say 'today', because such places are disappearing all the time beneath the sprawl of urban development, the deep waters of reservoirs and through the action of that age-old enemy of the deserted settlement site – the plough. Those that are scheduled as ancient monuments enjoy some protection, but the fate of other villages is as dependent on economic factors now as it was when they lived.

From our vantage point, we view a wider horizon, for the scope of this book is not restricted to those casualties

ABOVE: *Ruined 19th century cottages at Foggintor Quarry, Dartmoor.*
OPPOSITE: *St Mary's church, Houghton on the Hill.*

of the medieval and post-medieval periods, but delves further back into England's fascinating past, to rediscover settlements from as early as the Bronze Age through to the Saxon period. Also considered are the modern casualties of regional or national necessity, as well as those places that have succumbed to natural forces or the folly of men. There is no comprehensive gazetteer of lost villages, for such a document does not exist in a definitive form. Rescue digs for modern development sites frequently uncover traces of early communities, while a greater understanding of settlement types has removed some former candidates from the list.

Yet before we can take a closer look at the information encapsulated in these sites, we must first define what is meant by a 'lost' village. The debate over nomenclature has been raging since Beresford first published *The Lost Villages of England* – people pointed out that if he knew where these places were, they could no longer be called 'lost', prompting him to revise the term for 'Deserted Medieval Villages'. Even this description was not entirely accurate, however, as many of the settlements considered were not completely deserted, instead living on in the form of a single farmhouse or a hamlet of scattered cottages. Therefore, although no one has yet satisfactorily defined what actually constitutes a village, any settlement site where there are three inhabited houses or less is considered deserted. In the context of this book, the 'Lost' of our title should be interpreted as meaning the loss of the village community, rather than being confined to a count of dwellings, allowing us to include shrunken as well as shifted or migrated villages.

The importance of lost village sites as sources of information and insight into the daily lives of ordinary people from the past should not be underestimated. Their greatest value lies in their desertion, for as Professor Beresford once wrote, 'the dead cannot be easily sought among the living'.

INTRODUCTION

Good Heaven! What sorrows gloom'd that parting day,
That call'd them from their native walks away;
When the poor exiles, every pleasure past,
Hung round their bowers, and fondly looked their last…

OLIVER GOLDSMITH, *THE DESERTED VILLAGE*, 1770

At the time of its publication, Oliver Goldsmith's emotive account of an assault on the 'bold' English peasantry by greedy, self-aggrandizing landlords galvanized public opinion against the fashion for demolishing villages to make way for landscaped parkland around grand country houses. This 18th-century poem, which was based on first-hand experience of a rural depopulation, has since inspired a number of academics to take up the search for deserted medieval villages, an aim

BELOW: *A Luttrell Psalter (1345) illustration showing barley taken to a mill for grinding, typical food processing for the time.*

that has evolved into a quest to better understand the evolution of settlements in the English landscape from all periods.

However, the main upsurge of interest in the in-depth study of deserted settlements sprang from the 600th anniversary of the Black Death in 1949. Just three years earlier, the economic historian Sir John Clapham had declared that 'deserted villages are singularly rare in England', a belief shared by many historians at the time. Yet, by the 1950s, research published by pioneers in the study of 'lost' villages such as professors Maurice Beresford and W. G. Hoskins, was beginning to force a re-evaluation of the history of English rural settlements. They were joined in this groundbreaking endeavour by J. G. Hurst who, together with Beresford, founded the Deserted Medieval Village Research Group (today known as the Deserted Settlement Research Group).

Large-scale archaeological excavations followed at Wharram Percy, Yorkshire (see pages 150-151), Hound Tor, Devon (see pages 24-27), Upton, Gloucestershire (see pages 48-49), and Goltho in Linconshire. These studies advanced our understanding of the plan, form and mechanisms of medieval English villages. More recently, extensive work at Shapwick, Somerset, has continued that early scrutiny of medieval settlement structure and, aided by numerous smaller scale or 'rescue' digs, has furthered our knowledge about the development of the 'typical' English village. Deserted settlement sites are a very important resource in this regard, because their story is uninterrupted by subsequent development. They also preserve many aspects of the life of the medieval peasant, who by virtue of his lowly standing is largely absent from the written record.

Finding and examining evidence

To begin with, of course, there is the need to locate a 'lost' village. One of the most fascinating aspects of deserted settlement study is that it involves multi-disciplinary research, necessitating the co-operation of geographers, historians and archaeologists, often with invaluable assistance from amateur local historians. Lists of old villages have been compiled by scouring the earliest written sources, such as Saxon land charters and the immensely valuable material contained within William the Conqueror's comprehensive survey of 1086, subsequently

dubbed the Domesday Book, while later records, such as the 14th-century *Nomina Villarum*, can aid in the search for villages that developed in the 12th and 13th centuries. The names gathered are then painstakingly compared with modern maps and gazetteers to identify those that appear to be missing today. From this point, attempts to trace the histories of these 'lost' villages can be made through the examination of contemporary documents, such as the records of manorial administration and jurisdiction, rents, medieval taxation, lawsuits brought before the courts of Chancery and Exchequer, estate plans and land transfer transactions. A few of these sources, particularly those documents pertaining to taxation, allow rough estimates for the varying levels of a settlement's population to be calculated, which can then act as a useful framework when piecing together the sequence of events that led to depopulation. However, case studies such as that of Cold Newton, Leicestershire (see pages 123-124) have shown that desertion of the core village site and the resulting disintegration of community could still occur even when the number of residents stayed roughly the same. Many settlements were never individually listed; a parish of several communities was often used as the basic unit for administration. Still others may have been abandoned before the Norman Conquest. If we are lucky, complete records of a

ABOVE: *A small village with thatched roofs, the 'new' Milton Abbas was built in the 1780s to replace one that spoiled the view for Joseph Damer, owner of a large house in the area.*

depopulation can be found, as was the case at Wormleighton, Warwickshire (see pages 114-115), when events were documented in court transcripts, the result of Cardinal Wolsey's official inquiry into the actions of depopulating landlords from the late 15th and early 16th centuries. The story of Nuneham Courtenay, Oxfordshire, meanwhile, is related in the diary of its rector.

It is clear that the written record is at once valuable and limited in the search for lost village sites, and eventually reference to the physical landscape is required. An initial perusal of maps can sometimes yield useful results. The presence of an isolated church, a peculiar gap in the distribution of settlements, the unexplained convergence of several roads and tracks or the identity of a former settlement surviving in the name of a farm or other existing feature are all elements that can indicate a likely site. Yet some caution should be exercised, for in Northamptonshire, despite numerous local landmarks bearing 'Sulby' in their names, the 'lost' village itself was finally located at Park Farm (see pages 121-122). Moreover, a church seemingly stranded amid farmland,

ABOVE: *A reconstructed medieval cottage based on archaeological excavations of a village site at Hangleton, Sussex.*

and-white photographs are excellent at showing up the complete village plan of hollow-ways, house-platforms, boundary ditches and ridge and furrow cultivation, especially if these features happen to lie under a light dusting of snow, while vertical shots are particularly good at picking out the shadowy parch-marks that sometimes appear in vegetation growing across a site that has been completely ploughed-out, and of which no trace remains visible on the ground. The birds-eye view allows all the components to be seen at once, and can reveal spatial relationships not immediately apparent on the ground. Even so, painstaking field-surveys are still vital for mapping the contours of the earthworks, and for all the clarity of air photographs or excellent ground plans produced by surface exploration, the true nature and usage of the 'identified' elements can only be truly understood by careful excavation.

There is something uniquely satisfying about walking the paths of lost villages, and discovering that you are gradually able to hypothesize about the original form and purpose of the grassy undulations that surround you. Hollow-ways are probably the most easily recognizable features of a deserted village site. These are tracks worn down by the passage of man and beast through the ages, until their weathered, unmetalled surfaces fell well below the level of the adjacent land. Sometimes the plans of dwellings can be clearly read, especially if built after the 13th century when, as long as local stone was available, the walls of buildings became much more substantial and long-lasting. Earlier structures created with perishable materials, such as timber and turf or wattle and daub, may not have left pronounced profiles on top of the house site and yet their interiors may still show as hollowed depressions in the turf. A moated site may indicate a manor house, while a pronounced platform by a stream might once have supported a watermill. Windmill mounds are often found on high ground near the village, while rabbit warrens can sometimes be identified by a sequence of 'pillow' mounds. In areas where the land has been beneath pasture since desertion, the corrugations of ridge and furrow can still be made out, the former open fields being separated from the area of settlement by a ditch.

but perhaps situated near a large house, may well have started as a private chantry or chapel for the lord of the manor, therefore any search for a lost village in its vicinity is likely to prove fruitless. Thankfully, in the 19th century cartographers at the Ordnance Survey began noting earthworks, depicting their undulating profiles with hatched marks that were frequently labelled 'moats'. Modern maps are now more likely to bear the names of vanished villages that have been identified.

Field work and photography

A walking survey out in the field will often yield much useful information, and perhaps even identify a previously unknown site that may not immediately correspond to any on the lists of the missing. Sometimes only careful archaeological investigations can confirm if the lumps and bumps in a field do in fact represent the site of a lost village. For example, earthworks at Chartley, Staffordshire, were first believed to represent a settlement that had grown up in the shadow of the castle, but after further investigation, they now appear to be the result of gravel quarrying. Sadly, much in the way of genuine earthwork remains have been lost to the plough.

Perhaps one of the greatest aids to the search for lost villages has been the aerial photograph. Oblique black-

Boundaries, whether they ranged around the entire settlement or an individual croft, are probably the single oldest elements of all villages. Archaeological excavations have shown that a surprising amount of internal re-organization could occur within those confines, with buildings often changing location or orientation within the clearly defined area. Temporarily removing the protective layer of turf can also reveal the plans of these structures, which would range from the single-roomed cottage with its central open hearth, to longhouses, divided into living quarters and a byre, and the multi-chambered open-hall houses of the wealthier yeomen farmers.

ABOVE: *The ruined St Martin's Church is all that remains of the once-thriving village of Wharram Percy, Yorkshire.*

In addition, this process almost invariably brings to light artefacts and objects that can reveal much about the life of the former villagers. Animal bones, seeds and grains tell of livestock and cultivation as well as diet, while human bones speak of health and life expectancy. Pollen, molluscs and insects recovered can help to reconstruct the nature of the environment, telling us whether conditions were wet or dry, wooded or open plain. Perhaps most useful of all, fragments of pottery are commonly found, which can help us to work out the lifespan of the settlement. The absence of an item can also make a telling statement; compared to the large quantities of Roman coins regularly found on earlier sites, the medieval village seems to have relied on barter and exchange for most of its day to day transactions, as the discovery of coinage within the peasant properties is particularly rare.

Of course, the sites described above belong to the medieval or immediately post-medieval era, while villages have been abandoned in earlier periods and are still being deserted today. Around 100 lost towns and villages have been identified from the Saxon period, although there are undoubtedly many more, but the nature of their construction means that their discovery is often accidental, as very little of their fabric has survived, and buildings can only be identified by the dark circles of soil that represent the holes that once held the supporting timbers. The sites of more recent depopulations, meanwhile, need little in the way of interpretation, for they were very like their neighbours that survive today.

From prehistory to the present day, the reasons for depopulation are as many and varied as the villages themselves. It is rare, except in the more modern examples perhaps, for there to have been a single underlying cause; rather than a sudden exodus, the desertion of a settlement may well have taken several decades. More often, a combination of climatic deterioration, population pressure, disease and economic factors led to the demise of settlements. It has been noticed that many of the villages that failed to survive had always been less populous than others in the area, and a predisposing weakness can be detected in many of our subsequently 'lost' medieval villages. No corresponding weaknesses are detectable in the later depopulations, however, which were also distinctly more abrupt in nature. Quite often, however, they occurred in areas where the density of settlement was particularly low, and therefore the number of people affected by the creation of a reservoir or army training ground could be kept to a minimum. A fact that would no doubt be small comfort to the thousands of villagers over the centuries who, for one reason or another, have found themselves forced to search for an new place to call home.

THE SOUTH WEST

A region with some of the oldest lost villages, as well as some of the more recent, our tour of the south west takes us from the Late Neolithic period to the Second World War.

Carn Brea, on Cornwall's Land's End Peninsula, was occupied between around 3700 and 3400 BC, and provides the first evidence of permanent Neolithic settlement in Britain. With a possible population of between 100 to 150 people, it can lay claim to the title of earliest-known English village.

Saved from the worst of the medieval depopulations by a settlement pattern of dispersed hamlets and early enclosure, the lost villages of the far south west appear to have been the result of retreat from the high moorland zones during periods of deteriorating climate. Further east, there are signs of more widespread decline. In the early decades of the 14th century, an increasing amount of Gloucestershire arable land was deemed infertile, or lay 'frisc' (uncultivated). Pasture began to encroach on the open fields, and holdings remained vacant for want of tenants. It was not long before entire settlements were abandoned.

Later, almost 1,000 years after the Norman Conquest, the threat of invasion loomed once more as war in Europe became imminent. Among the ensuing casualties were two small villages from the south west of England: Imber and Tyneham.

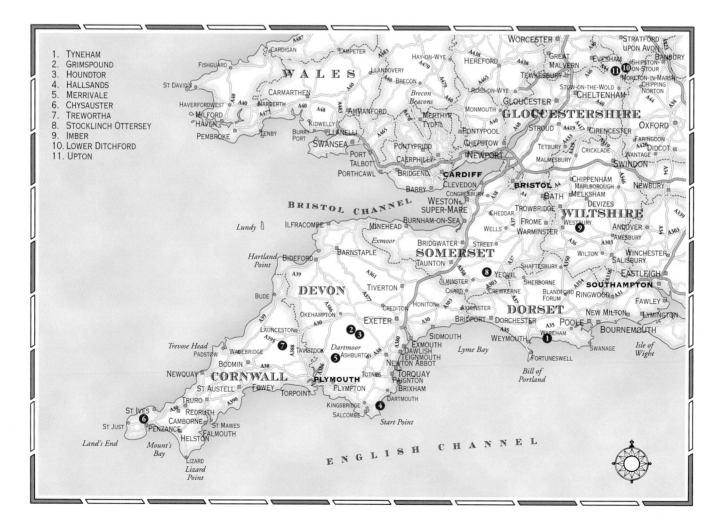

1. TYNEHAM
2. GRIMSPOUND
3. HOUNDTOR
4. HALLSANDS
5. MERRIVALE
6. CHYSAUSTER
7. TREWORTHA
8. STOCKLINCH OTTERSEY
9. IMBER
10. LOWER DITCHFORD
11. UPTON

TYNEHAM
DORSET

ABOVE
Brightly painted, yet sealed shut, the old phonebox on Post Office Row still has wartime notices pasted within its interior.

ABOVE
The village as it was in 1930, just over a decade before news of the planned evacuation reached the villagers.

PREVIOUS PAGE
The ruins of cottages at Foggintor, once possibly inhabited by an early 20th-century quarrying community.

A row of rustic thatched cottages stands in the shadow of a square-towered village church, while a ragged group of militant labourers dressed in early 19th-century garb – the founders of the Friendly Society of Agricultural Workers – gathers in earnest conversation beneath the tall elm on the green. Yet the year is not 1833 but 1985, and the place – not Tolpuddle but another well-known Dorset village some miles distant: Tyneham. Depopulated at a time of national emergency, this once-attractive yet hard-working village stands empty and ruinous amid a vast army training area. So faithfully does Tyneham represent a centuries-old rural landscape that it has on occasion found itself dressed as a set for television or film productions. One such production was *Comrades*, Bill Douglas's 1985 film about the Tolpuddle Martyrs, for which a mature tree was planted on the green, and a fake church tower quickly constructed. Yet for most of the time, Tyneham is empty and silent, save for scurrying wildlife and the persistent crump of guns.

Our first glimpse of early Tyneham came in 1859, with the excavation of an Iron-Age industrial site and settlement there. More than 2,000 years ago, the local Kimmeridge shale stone was worked by people of the Dwr y Trges (Durotriges) tribe to create amulets, bracelets and necklaces, personal ornaments later admired by the Romans; in fact, both settlement and industry flourished during the occupation. Yet, surrounded as it is by numerous relics of prehistory, this valley was clearly favoured long before the shale-workers took up residence. Bounded by gently rolling hills in all landward directions, and to the south by the sea, the isolation of this compact coastal location is one factor that attracted the army in 1942 when, in order to train British and American tank crews for the planned assault on Normandy's beaches, it sought to expand its existing gunnery ranges at Lulworth. Unfortunately, the use of live ordnance made it imperative that the tiny village that lay at the heart of this new battle training ground should be evacuated.

Those final Tyneham residents long maintained that assurances were given that their removal from the village was merely a temporary precaution, and that once hostilities ceased, they would be allowed to regain possession of their homes. As tenants of the Bond family, who held the Tyneham estate (and therefore much of the parish), the villagers did not actually own any of the properties. Consequently, when it became clear that the government intended to retain the land indefinitely, the ordinary folk of Tyneham merely received compensation for the produce of their gardens. Nevertheless, as far as the villagers were concerned, Tyneham, while not their property, was certainly their home, and had been for many years – in a number of cases, for generations.

Since the evacuation, a great deal has been written about Tyneham, much of it penned by former residents; memoirs often criticised – by both outsiders and former villagers – for painting too idyllic a picture of life there. For we are presented with an enchanting scene of a remote and peaceful valley blessed with a temperate climate; a pest-free sanctuary for flora and fauna, where snow rarely fell. And of a village where the men still habitually dressed in traditional smocks made from home-grown flax, and where iron-hooped wooden buckets were still carried on yokes. Wistful nostalgia aside, these first-hand stories provide a fascinating account of a virtually self-sufficient community that spoke a language almost of its own, and lived a now vanished way of life.

Village life

Run along lines of almost feudal interdependence between the landowning employer and his tenant labourers, the estate and village were directed from Tyneham House. A gabled, three-storey Elizabethan mansion of grey Purbeck ashlar built in 1523, it boasted grand mullioned windows that looked out upon colourful gardens, immaculate lawns and a majestic avenue of lime trees. One of the three great houses on the Isle of Purbeck, it had been home to the Bond family since 1683. Included within its complex of outbuildings was an even earlier manor house dating from the 14th century.

The village itself largely comprised a single street of scattered grey stone cottages and the medieval church of St Mary, a small cruciform-plan building built of limestone rubble. Refurbished in the late 18th century, the church interior contained the splendid monuments of the Bond family in Caen stone. At harvest festival, the church would

be beautifully decorated with flowers and vegetables from the gardens of Tyneham House, and it was not an uncommon sight for wild and domestic animals to invade the services to which all had been called by two modest bells hung in an exterior bell-cote.

Close by stood the early 19th-century single-roomed National School, which, together with the rectory, was one of the few substantial buildings in the village. Further along, in a line of terraced cottages known locally as The Row, stood the village bakery, which eventually became the General Store, with the later addition of a Post Office,

ABOVE
A crumbling Post Office and a lone phonebox are all that is left of the once vibrant thoroughfare known as Post Office Row.

where Tyneham's only telephone could be found (until a phone box was installed shortly before evacuation). There was no village inn, the nearest pub being the Ragged Cat, which was some distance away on the Lulworth Road. Entertainment came in the curious form of itinerant Italian organ grinders with their trained animals, performing bears and travelling thespians, although the Bond children did produce local amateur theatrical events in the great barn at Tyneham Farm.

From the village, a small winding path lined with local fishermen's cottages followed a small stream called the Gwyle as it dropped 0.8km (0.5 miles) through a narrow valley to the sea at Worbarrow Bay. Sharing only the church, schoolroom and Post Office with the rest of the village, the fisherfolk of Worbarrow were almost a self-contained community. From the communal effort of hauling the nets full of mackerel onto the beach, to the making of crab and lobster pots, every man, woman and child played their part. It was said that none of the men ever learned to swim, their philosophy being that if you were destined to drown it was better to get it over with quickly. They were clearly not averse to taking risks as smuggling formed a lucrative sideline, the contraband being stored in an inaccessible cave in neighbouring Brandy Bay before being moved to a bramble-covered cave in Tyneham Wood for onward distribution.

Above all, the Tyneham estate relied on mixed arable and livestock farming. The estate's 700 sheep, each with its own bell, were watched over by a single shepherd and his dog. There was also abundant pasture for dairy cattle, the milk being sent to London by train from nearby Corfe. No fences prevented the animals from wandering onto the rough gravel tracks that passed for roads, but a multitude of gates would restrict their movements, while the fields around the village were lined with grey stone walls and separated by quick-set hedges, patched with small woods and coppices or belts of trees – formations essential to the success of the shooting parties regularly held at Tyneham House. Across this landscape, the horse provided the necessary motive force up until 1937, when tractors were introduced.

It was on the bitterly cold day of 17 November 1943, as the village began its traditional preparations for the forthcoming festive season, that the Creech village postmaster delivered to every household the letters that brought the unwelcome news of evacuation. The date set for the military takeover was 19 December. By that time, nearly half of the Isle of Purbeck had been requisitioned, and the gunnery ranges at Lulworth expanded. In addition, an RAF radar station sat atop the lofty Tyneham Cap; women from the WAAF (Women's Auxiliary Air Force) were billeted at Tyneham House, and airmen lodged in the village. Barbed wire had become a familiar sight in the landscape, as had the tank traps along the coast.

A village in exile

Villagers who had already given so much for their country (the parish had lost many young men in the Great War) patriotically did their duty and peacefully accepted the eviction, buoyed by the belief that they would be back before the hay was due to be harvested. Temporary accommodation and alternative employment were found, and gradually the village emptied. Within weeks, this tight-knit community had been scattered across the Isle of Purbeck, yet the people's thoughts never strayed far from home, and most were simply marking time until the end of the war. But sadly, the end of hostilities in 1945 did not bring about the end of their exile. Frustrated and concerned, Tyneham's villagers wrote to the War Office, dismayed at the deteriorating condition of their cottages, the overgrown fields and shell-damaged church. As time went by, they intensified the pressure until finally, in 1947, the news broke that the parish of Tyneham-cum-Steeple was to be retained by compulsory purchase to become part of a 7,200-acre (2,880-hectare) gunnery range.

Though impassioned protests brought about a public enquiry, a government White Paper made it clear that, while some promises may have been made regarding the eventual return of Tyneham, it was necessary for all personal considerations to be overridden by what was in the best interests of the nation. As any last hope of returning home vanished for the villagers, many were offered the chance to be rehoused at Sandford, near Wareham, in a small estate of newly built council houses known as Tyneham Close. Light and modern, with electricity and indoor plumbing, these dwellings were a world away from the draughty old stone cottages of the village, with their antiquated sanitation. A number of former Tyneham folk were quite content in their new homes, but many others, broken-hearted, never really recovered from the shock. Yet even they were eventually forced to concede that there was by now little left of the old Tyneham to move back to.

Interest in the village never waned, however. The demise of the great Tyneham House, demolished by the Ministry of Works in the 1960s, brought renewed protests. Candlelit vigils were held by pressure groups intent on gaining greater access to the village, with the result that firing is now halted on certain specially designated days of the year, allowing visitors to the village. A special car park has been built, and picnic tables installed. Moreover, the old school has been set up as though the children have merely stepped outside for a moment, while the church, restored and now maintained by the army, houses an exhibition chronicling both the history of the village and the current importance of the area as a protected natural habitat. In 1975, the graveyard was restored and used for burials once more.

With its gravestones scoured clean and

its pond freshly dug out, many feel that the village has become sanitized, its unique character lost. And yet this ghost village still exerts a powerful attraction, having attained a mythical status in the public's imagination. Visiting Tyneham today, one recalls the parting plea pinned to the church door by the villagers as they stoically vacated their homes for the national good. Their haunting words are now famous: 'Please treat the church and houses with care; we have given up our homes where many of us lived for generations to help win the war to keep men free. We shall return one day and thank you for treating the village kindly.'

ABOVE
The Gardener's Cottage is presently undergoing renovation.

OPPOSITE, TOP
The gable end of the Rectory.

OPPOSITE, BOTTOM
Fallen cottage floors have resulted in 'elevated' fireplaces.

GRIMSPOUND
DARTMOOR, DEVON

ABOVE
A view of a circular enclosure from atop the lofty Hookney Tor.

BELOW
A rock formation thought to be the original single gateway to the Bronze Age settlement of Grimspound. The remains of the steps and paving are visible.

Beautiful yet treacherous, inhospitable yet strewn with the remnants of 5,000 years of human habitation, the 950 square kilometres (365 square miles) of Dartmoor National Park present an enigmatic combination of the picturesque and the mysterious. Of the many thousands of ancient landmarks scattered throughout the area, including burial mounds, stone rows and hut circles, perhaps the best known and undoubtedly the most evocative is the lost village of Grimspound.

To obtain the best views of this settlement, one must climb up to the lofty vantage point of Hookney Tor. From there, a massive but somewhat dilapidated circular wall of granite boulders can be clearly picked out amid the bracken and heather on the slopes below. Within this 1.5-hectare (4-acre) enclosure, 24 stone hut circles and a handful of inner paddock banks appear as an irregular pattern of large stones scattered amongst the encroaching vegetation, while a small stream, the Grimslake, flows along its northern boundary. If present 3,500 years ago, when the settlement was occupied, this tiny watercourse could have constituted the village's water supply.

The name Grimspound, first recorded and published by the Reverend Richard Polwhele in 1797, has an otherworldly association that seems somehow fitting in this setting renowned for legend and superstition. Many believe the name to derive from that of the Anglo-Saxon god Grim, also known as Woden, or as Odin, the Norse god of war. Alternatively, it can mean 'savage' – a reflection perhaps on the sometimes cruel nature of the environment in these high, desolate reaches of moorland – or it may even refer to the mythological leader of the wild hunt. There have also been suggestions that in Old English, the word denotes a place whose method of, or reason for, construction had been long forgotten and was therefore, for want of a better explanation, associated with the work of the Devil. Unfortunately, we will never know what the village was called by its inhabitants.

The climate on Dartmoor was once significantly kinder than it is today, and the people who lived in the village's thatched roundhouses may well have been able to grow a limited range of crops in small garden patches within the compound. However, they are likely to have been predominantly cattle farmers, trading their beasts for grain and tools. Situated in an indefensible position overlooked by two great tors, the double wall of the outer perimeter, measuring 1–1.5m (3–5 feet) high and 3m (9 feet)

wide in places, may have been topped with a sturdy wooden palisade, and was no doubt intended to keep the livestock in and predators such as wolves and bears out. The compound's single main entrance opened onto an uphill track, along which the livestock would have been driven to graze during the day. An impressive stepped pavement helped to make the gradient manageable, while the entrance itself was defined by several very large stones. It is probable that a heavy wooden barrier would have been fixed firmly across the 2-m (6.5-foot) wide gap when the animals had all been corralled safely. A short distance to the southeast of the compound lie the remains of four enclosures, possibly fields bounded by granite rubble walling, along with nine further stone hut circles.

Excavation and reconstruction

During the course of an extensive excavation of the site by the Dartmoor Exploration Committee in 1894, a number of the hut circles were investigated and partially rebuilt. At the same time, a section of the outer wall was also reconstructed. It is therefore fortunate that a highly accurate survey of the site had been carried out 65 years earlier by A. C. Shillibear, recording the archaeological remains as they appeared prior to the subsequent disturbances. Yet for all the exhaustive work undertaken in 1894, little was found in the way of artefacts – just a small amount of pottery was recovered, together with a handful of flint implements and some cooking stones. Even so, thirteen of the huts yielded evidence of human occupation, with sleeping platforms, hearth stones or cooking pits, while the rest was of simpler construction, and was interpreted as animal pens or store houses.

Archaeological techniques at the end of the 19th century were not as sophisticated and painstaking as they are today. As a consequence, much of significance is likely to have been lost at Grimspound. It may be some time before a thorough investigation of the remaining, as yet unexcavated, areas of the site is made, so we can only speculate as to the number of associated timber structures that could also have existed there.

ABOVE
One of the many circles of granite boulders found at Grimspound. These enclosures are known as 'hut circles' or 'round houses'.

It is possible to make an informed guess regarding roof construction, however, because contemporary structures have been excavated elsewhere, suggesting that the roofs were probably conical in shape, thatched with either bracken, heather or turf over branches, and supported by a large central wooden post. The huts themselves had a double skin of stones standing 1m (3 feet) high, the gap in between perhaps being filled with turf as additional protection against the elements. The bare earth floors were dug out to maximize the headroom, and were just 3.5m (11.5 feet) across on average. Sheltered by a curved porch, the paved entrance opened downhill, away from the prevailing winds. With furs, hides, dried grass, bracken or heather upholstering the interior, life around the hearth might have been quite snug, albeit somewhat cramped.

Yet no amount of precautions could defend the community's livelihood against a steadily deteriorating climate. Towards the end of the Bronze Age, conditions gradually worsened. Increased rainfall leached the goodness from the thin soils, and crops failed to ripen during the duller, overcast summers; the steady loss of grazing land under peat was an additional problem. At some point, the farming families of Grimspound gave up the struggle and joined the steady retreat down into the valleys. Since that time, the roofless and crumbling huts have provided temporary shelter for shepherds and tin-streamers, not to mention a famous fictional character. Sherlock Holmes hid in a prehistoric hut in *The Hound of the Baskervilles*, the inspiration for which can almost certainly be found amid the ruins of Grimspound.

It was the Dartmoor Exploration Committee that first brought Grimspound to the public's attention, finally dispelling the myth that it had once been a temple of the Druids. More than a century later, the preservation work is now in the hands of English Heritage. Although Grimspound can be quite tricky to find without a guide or a good Ordnance Survey map, its remains are ample reward for the effort.

RIGHT
This hut circle, with Hookney Tor in the distance, is one of perhaps as many as 5,000 hut circles scattered across Dartmoor.

HOUNDTOR
DARTMOOR, DEVON

ABOVE
The remains of the deserted medieval village of Hundatora lie in the distance, just beyond the rocks of Hound Tor.

On the slopes below the weathered, grey granite stacks of Dartmoor's Hound Tor, which rise 448m (1,469 feet) above sea level, lie the stone foundations of Hundatora (Houndtor). Perhaps the largest – and certainly the best known – of the moor's deserted medieval villages, the site was first occupied 2,300 to 4,000 years ago during the Bronze Age. By then, deliberate burning had significantly reduced the oak and hazel woodland that once clothed the upper reaches of Dartmoor, expanding the small patches of open heath around the high tors into productive grazing and farmland.

Human alteration and management of the landscape continued apace with the development of 'reave' systems. These divided much of the moor into large enclosures bounded by low, earth-covered stone banks, and enabled the supervision of livestock as well as the cultivation of cereals. During the last millennium BC, however, these pioneering farmers were forced down from the upper reaches of the moor as cooler, wetter conditions reduced the amount of grazing for their sheep, cattle and ponies. Higher rainfall accelerated the leaching of the thin soil, already exhausted by centuries of intensive cultivation, resulting in waterlogged and acidic land.

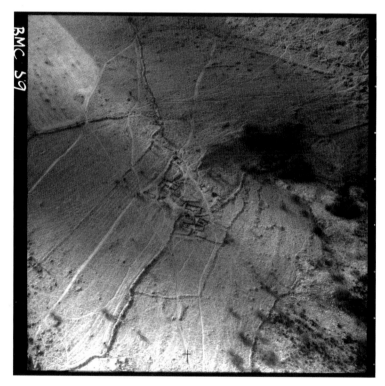

There are few tangible remnants of early occupation on the high moor, but the improving climate of the late Saxon period encouraged the resettlement of its valleys and fringes. By the 10th century AD, new farming settlements and associated field systems were being established. One, with spectacular views over the Lustleigh valley, was the classic upland village of Hundatora. Sheltered from the prevailing winds, it developed as a haphazard cluster of huts and outbuildings, each dwelling sitting within its own small garden plot, while above the village could be found large irregular 'infields' of oats and rye. Beyond these collectively farmed terraces were the 'outfields' – land that was only occasionally cultivated, and which often merged with the surrounding bracken-covered open moorland.

ABOVE
Eleven seperate structures are discernable from the air as all that remain of Houndtor.

OPPOSITE
Hawthorn scrub appears to be slowly reclaiming the site that was once the village of Houndtor.

The medieval longhouse

Archaeological excavation in the 1960s revealed traces of a number of early dwellings with hollowed-out floors and thick turf walls encased in a retaining outer shell of wattle hurdles. The complex sequence of stake holes uncovered suggests frequent renewal, perhaps even rebuilding, initially at least, on roughly the same alignment as the previous structure. Then the pattern changed abruptly, with a shift through 90°, a development now thought to relate to the introduction of a new type of upland farm dwelling known as a longhouse, in which the people and their animals all lived under the same thatched roof.

Originally just a single storey in height, a medieval longhouse was a long, low building, with its two interior rooms open to the roof. In the living area, there was a cooking pit of hot ash, as well as a central hearth. Without the aid of a chimney, smoke from the fire would drift

up into and percolate out through the thatch, although wattle-and-daub smoke 'hoods' were sometimes constructed to help it on its way. A central cross-passage with a wooden doorway at each end separated the living area from the 'shippon', where the animals (cattle and possibly sheep) were housed. It was therefore essential, principally for reasons of drainage, that these large multi-purpose structures should be built against rather than across the slope of a hill, as had previously been the custom, with the byres always situated at the lower end. Over time, some of the Houndtor longhouses appear to have gained porches, and sleeping platforms, accessible by ladders, may also have been added.

There continues to be some debate about whether the turf-walled structures generally preceded the stone buildings at Houndtor, as well as uncertainty over the degree to which a change in building material can be said to reflect the deterioration in climatic conditions after the comparatively warm 11th and 12th centuries. Nevertheless, we can be sure that what we see today are the well-preserved foundations of structures constructed, at least in part, of roughly coursed granite boulders, sometime during the 13th century. These buildings appear to have had walls up to 1.8m (6 feet) in height, but few, if any, small windows, in an attempt, perhaps, to retain the heat.

Eleven separate structures have been identified in the medieval village of Houndtor. The largest may have represented some form of manor house, while three were longhouses measuring approximately 15m (50 feet) long by 4m (14 feet) wide, some with later additions and modifications to the original basic plan. As well, there were four smaller cottages, with the later construction of three substantial corn-drying barns, each containing a pair of kilns of a type commonly found on high, marginal land, where the damper conditions caused by altitude would have made natural drying difficult. Circular in form and raised on stone platforms, these large kilns could have been used to dry anything from peas to hay. As conditions grew colder and wetter in the 14th century, the arable portion of the village's mixed farming economy would have come to depend on these structures.

The final years

Composed largely of impervious granite, subject to high rainfall and with a climate dominated by southwesterly winds, Dartmoor is generally cool and wet underfoot. Therefore, the discovery of charred oats during the excavation of one of the drying kilns at Houndtor was hardly a surprise. Oats, tolerant of cold, damp conditions, also produced vitally nutritious straw, and so probably became the crop of choice during the settlement's difficult final years. Even so, as the climate steadily worsened, the strain on the village economy grew. Harvests from the thin, waterlogged soil became unreliable, and efforts

to find sufficient winter feed grew more desperate. Then, when the situation on Dartmoor must have been looking very bleak indeed, the scattered farmsteads and small villages of Devon found their populations reduced by up to two-thirds as the Black Death (1348–50) swept the land. In most cases, however, it is unlikely that the major depopulating factor was the pestilence itself. Instead, it was probably the lure of numerous newly available, fertile holdings elsewhere that resulted in the abandonment of so many marginal settlements in the mid-14th century.

Often shrouded in mist and occasionally treacherous due to its numerous hidden bogs and other dangers, Dartmoor has long been regarded as an eerily mysterious, otherworldly place. A rich tradition of superstition and folklore has evolved there, much of it concerning the Devil, who, on particularly wild nights, is said to roam across the wilderness. One legend recalls an early medieval bowman called Bowerman who was out on the moor with his hounds when he encountered a group of witches (or some say the Devil himself), and was immediately transformed into a tower of granite, while

one of his hapless dogs, similarly cursed, became Houndtor. It is claimed that this local story was the inspiration for Sir Arthur Conan Doyle's famous novel, *The Hound of the Baskervilles*, and several dramatized versions have been filmed there.

Thanks to its ecological importance and outstanding beauty, Dartmoor enjoys a measure of protection as a national park. Located within the park boundaries, Houndtor is in the care of the Secretary of State for Culture, Media and Sport, although responsibility for the site's maintenance has been delegated to the park authorities. The deserted village is readily accessible because of its proximity to a minor road. Unfortunately, its large numbers of visitors have inevitably had an impact on the site. Over the years, several of the medieval walls have crumbled, resulting in their somewhat haphazard 'reconstruction'. Now, however, the park has embarked on a programme to put this right. Photographs from the archaeological excavations in the 1960s are being used to restore the ruins as far as possible, their stones being glued in place with epoxy resin.

ABOVE
The outbuildings of the Houndtor longhouses, such as the one above, were used for a variety of purposes, including the housing of kilns used for drying corn.

HALLSANDS

DEVON

ABOVE
Only the gable end of this old Hallsands house still stands.

BELOW
Hallsands village before the final destructive storm, sheltering behind newly built seawalls.

ABOVE
Only the gable end of this old Hallsands house still stands.

BELOW
Hallsands village before the final destructive storm, sheltering behind newly built seawalls.

During the night of 26 January, 1917, a ferocious storm hit the south Devon coast. By morning, the small fishing village of Hallsands had been swept into the sea. Many believe that this was a man-made tragedy, entirely preventable; others argue that the demise of this tiny settlement, wedged precariously onto a narrow ledge at the foot of precipitous cliffs, was a natural phenomenon. Whatever the truth of the matter, it was the people of Hallsands, all of whom thankfully survived the devastation of their village, that were left to try to piece back together the life of a community that had, until that moment, endured for centuries.

Just over 100 years ago, Hallsands was one of many hard-working fishing villages dotted around Start Bay. This was a stretch of coastline notorious for winter storms, but Hallsands sat snug against the bluff on a stretch of flat rock, safely above the high-tide mark and protected from the waves by a large pebble beach. With an economy based entirely on fishing, the village prospered and expanded in the 18th and 19th centuries, so that by 1891 it comprised 37 tightly packed houses (homes for around 160 people), served by a single narrow road. At the northern end of the village stood the old London Inn; there was also a post office, a grocery shop and, perched as a beacon high on the clifftop above, a chapel, with origins in the early 16th century.

It was a hard life, but one in which the entire village was involved. Hauling seine nets full of struggling fish up onto the shingle beach required the combined strength of every available man, woman and child. Many hands would then be needed to sort the catch. The best fish was packed and sent to London by rail, while lesser specimens might be used as bait for the locally made crab pots. In fact, crabbing was the mainstay of the economy here, the contents of the pots generally being harvested from well smacks. Such was the life of this community, with its intimate understanding of the winds, waves and tides upon which survival depended.

Dredging and damage

In 1896, the Admiralty ordered the extension of the Keyham dockyard at Devonport, Plymouth, some 50km (30 miles) distant from Hallsands. This vast concrete construction called for enormous quantities of sand and gravel, materials that could be found in abundance beneath the clear blue waters of Start Bay. A prominent engineering firm of the day won the contract, and its proprietor, Sir John Jackson, quickly obtained a licence from the Board of Trade permitting the extraction of sand, shingle and gravel from the seabed opposite the villages of Hallsands and Beesands.

It is evident that at no point were the local fishermen consulted or informed of this planned extraction, for in April 1897, when dredgers entered Start Bay for the first time, immediate protests were made by the inhabitants of both villages. Concern was voiced about the disturbance of the fishing grounds and possible damage to crab pots. Perhaps the overriding worry was that interfering with the natural composition of the bay was in some way dangerous. The Board of Trade may already have considered this possibility, as a clause in the extractor's licence allowed for instant revocation should the operation begin to threaten the coastline.

At a public inquiry held in April 1897, representatives of Sir John Jackson reassured everyone that there was no cause for alarm, arguing that the natural action of the sea would fill any holes with sand. We now know that the shingle protecting the beaches at Hallsands and Beesands had been deposited many thousands of years earlier during successive ice ages, but unaware of this fact and having conducted his own enquiries, the inspector found in favour of the extractors, although he recommended that all dredging activity be kept away from the beaches of the villages. Subsequently, Sir John agreed to pay the people of Hallsands £125 annually in compensation for the disruption to fishing, and pledged payment for repairs to damaged equipment.

In 1900, official complaints by the local parish council were renewed. Distinct changes had been detected in the pebble ridge that protected the village from the action of waves, and a second official inspection was ordered. Just as the local people had predicted, the level of the beach was found to have fallen. Action was immediately taken to restrict the activities of the

dredgers, but it was already too late: when the autumn storms arrived, part of the seawall crumbled. It was now feared that the houses themselves were also at risk. Meanwhile, Sir John continued to deny that his operations could be the cause of the problems, but offered to pay for any damage proven directly attributable to the dredging; he also provided new concrete foundations for the undermined seawall.

Following a complaint of damage to the road, another Board of Trade inspector arrived at Hallsands in March 1901. He

ABOVE
Cottages that sat right up against the rock face have now been reduced to little more than piles of rubble.

ABOVE

A view from the beach of a row of ruined cottages. As a result of dredging, the beach level in 1901 was found to have dropped in some places by as much as 3.5m (12 feet).

protests going unheeded, sabotaged the extraction operation by hauling the dredger buoys ashore. It would be another eight months before Hallsands' fishermen also became militant and all dredging ceased, the licence finally having been revoked. By this time, around 650,000 tons of material had been extracted from Start Bay.

At first it seemed that the beach might recover, but storms that winter caused more damage. In February 1903, the seawall protecting the London Inn was breached, part of it being washed away, while a similar scenario was unfolding at the other end of the village. There, part of the road and a slipway were destroyed, with one house seriously damaged. In bad weather, high tides now reached the most seaward of the houses. Before long, six houses had been completely destroyed, and others were in need of urgent repair. One corner of the London Inn was undermined, and several of its walls collapsed, with reports of water flying in the air to heights of 9–12m (30–40 feet).

A brief respite

Compensation of £3000 was offered by the Board of Trade and Sir John Jackson, but only on the condition that no further claims would be made. This inadequate sum had to be shared between those who were now homeless, plus pay for a substantial new seawall, the old walls having been totally destroyed. The beach had now shrunk 6m (19 feet) below its original height, making fishing more difficult as boats could no longer be securely beached, but the village's impressive new sea defences brought some much-needed respite. Behind the wall, the community made its repairs and simply carried on as best it could. There was a renewed sense of security and a return to some degree of normality for the brave people of Hallsands.

Sadly, the calm was not to last. The great storm of January 1917 happened to coincide with a particularly high tide. That night, gale-force winds drove waves crashing over the almost non-existent pebble ridge; the seawall was breached and icy water poured onto the houses. As the

quickly confirmed that the height of the beach had dropped, possibly by as much as 3.5m (12 feet) in places, and warned that flooding and serious damage to property were likely. His recommendation was that dredging should be stopped immediately. In several places the foundations of walls were now exposed, and new seawalls were necessary to protect the London Inn and other parts of the village from high tides. A few months later, part of the undercliff road disappeared, and the high-water mark was edging ominously closer to the rocky ledge upon which the village was built.

But still, dredging continued, until the fishermen of Beesands, tired of their

villagers fled to higher ground, roofs came crashing down, walls crumbled and belongings were washed out to sea. By midnight, four houses had gone. People looked on helplessly as one by one their homes collapsed into the bay. Finally, they were able to scramble up the narrow cliff path to the relative safety of higher ground, carrying with them whatever they had been able to salvage from their properties. The following day, their foundations severely undermined by the relentless action of the thundering waves, all but one of the remaining houses succumbed to the next high tide. In less than 24 hours, 29 homes had been completely destroyed.

The villagers were thankful to have escaped with their lives, although most had lost everything. Many found temporary lodgings; a few attempted to live in the remains of the least-damaged properties, but this was possible only in the summer months. It was several years before the legal arguments about culpability were resolved. The findings of the inquiry have never been published, but the Board accepted responsibility and a final compensatory figure of £6000 was agreed. In 1919, the villagers shared this money, as before, with a significant proportion earmarked for the building of new homes, this time on the clifftop.

Exactly how long Hallsands might have survived without the misguided interference with its shoreline remains uncertain. While there is little doubt that the removal of a huge amount of material from the seabed was a significant factor in the tragedy that befell the village, it is now thought that it merely accelerated a natural trend. Today, with the ruins of Hallsands in a dangerous state, public access is restricted. Holidaymakers and walkers following the South Devon Coastal Path must gaze down on the shells of crumbling dwellings from a clifftop viewing platform constructed by South Hams Council.

ABOVE
Even at the replacement village of North Hallsands, some cottages have suffered a watery demise.

ABOVE
An incomplete apple or gorse crushing stone discovered within one of the enclosures at Merrivale.

MERRIVALE
DEVON

Travel east from Tavistock along the B3357 and you will encounter a tiny hamlet that seems to exist in the middle of nowhere. There, situated opposite a small quarry, is the Dartmoor Inn, which sells the aptly named Merrivale Ale, for this is the site referred to in guidebooks as 'the Merrivale Antiquities'.

The megalithic complex at Merrivale is one of Dartmoor's most accessible archaeological sites, its main attractions being two long, double stone rows that align east to west along the crest of a ridge. It is an impressive prehistoric landscape of stone circles, standing stones, burial cairns and cists where, 4,000 years ago, people would have gathered to celebrate and worship. Some features have been badly damaged and plundered over the years, particularly in the early 19th-century, when road builders broke up the more accessible and portable stones to use as hardcore. Nevertheless, what remains exerts a powerful fascination over all who stand among these lichen-painted granite rocks that sparkle with quartz. Today, Merrivale is an unpopulated and peaceful landscape, the silence broken only by the sound of a small leat that rushes along between the stone rows.

BELOW
This 18th-century direction marker would help travellers find their way across the moor. The 'A' stands for Ashburton.

A Bronze Age colony

Things were very different in the Middle Bronze Age (*c.* 1800–1500 BC). The climate was warmer than it is today, allowing for the widespread colonization of the high moor. To the north, and set slightly apart from the ritual landscape, lies an area of settlement that remains visible as a sizeable cluster of 37 stone hut circles. It seems likely that they supplanted earlier timber huts, however no trace of these, or any other wooden structures that may once have stood here, has survived the intervening millennia. Situated on the gentle west-facing slopes of Long Ash Hill 350m (1,148 feet) above sea level, the settlement commands breathtaking views of the surrounding tors and valleys; Bodmin Moor forms the western horizon.

Often cloaked in thick Dartmoor mists that can lift as swiftly as they descend, the settlement occupied 4.5 hectares (11 acres). With walls that would once have reached a height of about 1m (3 feet), the huts were terraced into the hillside so that their interiors were level, and ranged from just over 2m (6 feet) to just over 9m (30 feet) in diameter. The smaller structures were perhaps store houses, byres or workshops, with the larger buildings forming the accommodations. Six of the stone hut circles were excavated by the Dartmoor Excavation Committee in the late 19th century, when it was discovered that two contained identifiable hearthstones, and another two had been paved. The dry-stone walls of the huts had an average width of 1.4m (4.6 feet), many being formed of a double ring of stones with rubble infill. South-facing entrances flanked by large stone door jambs would have led to a spacious interior beneath a thick roof of heather, gorse or reed thatch, that rested on a wooden framework supported in turn by a ring of posts and perhaps a central upright.

Among the huts, and probably post-dating them, were four roughly rectangular enclosures bounded by stone banks 1.5m (5 feet) wide and 0.6m (2 feet) high. It is not known what they were used for, but the predominance of natural bedrock at the surface makes crop cultivation seem unlikely. A far more plausible explanation is that these enclosures were crew yards for a community whose economy was based on rearing livestock. While the essential needs of the Bronze Age villagers were met by domestic cows, sheep and goats, and supplemented by wild plants and animals, cereals and beans may have been acquired as a result of trade. Pottery and flint tools not manufactured at the site could also have been obtained in this way.

The area covered by this settlement was probably far larger than it appears today, as further remains can be seen on the edge of Long Ash Common. In about 1500 BC, long stone boundary banks were constructed that separated enclosed rectilinear field systems from the open moor, built perhaps as a response to the change in climate as winters became wetter and summers cooler, necessitating greater management of dwindling resources. Even so, it was a battle the inhabitants of Merrivale could not win, and by 1000 BC, the abandonment of Dartmoor's higher reaches had begun.

Although never densely populated again, the area remained in use. In 1625 Merrivale earned the soubriquet 'Plague Market' or 'Potato Market', as it was used as a place of exchange between traders, farmers and the citizens of the plague-ridden town of Tavistock. Provisions were left on the site and payment collected from a receptacle filled with vinegar, thought at the time to be an antiseptic. There is also evidence that the area was used as a vast rabbit warren in medieval times. Numerous segmented 'pillow mounds' have been found, and the dry-stone walls of a warrener's cottage, built in 1830, can also be seen. Today, the area is used as pasture for livestock.

Much of the site is now a Scheduled Ancient Monument and, along with Houndtor (see pages 24–27) and Grimspound (see pages 20–23), it is the subject of a local management agreement between English Heritage and the Dartmoor National Park Authority.

BELOW
With more than 75 stone rows on Dartmoor, the ones at Merrivale are unique in that they run almost parallel with each other. Their use was probably ceremonial.

CHYSAUSTER
CORNWALL

ABOVE
The Iron Age village of Chysauster as seen from the air.

BELOW
The rows of stone-built courtyard houses at Chysauster would once have had thatched roofs.

Five kilometres (three miles) to the north of Penzance, on a gentle southwestern slope of the high granite uplands, two short rows of stone-walled houses with neat terraced gardens make up one of the oldest streets in England. Though no longer sporting their picturesque yet practical roofs of thatch or turf, the rooms and courtyards still reverberate with the sound of human voices – not the conversations of resident villagers, but rather the observations of visitors, for this remarkable little Cornish village, known today as Chysauster, has been uninhabited for around 1,700 years.

About 14km (9 miles) distant, another abandoned settlement of similar form, Carn Euny, has been dated by archaeologists to the late Iron Age. Established in around 200 BC, it was populated, adapted and rebuilt over a period of around 700 years. Chysauster itself is surrounded by an extensive system of ancient tracks and small fields, the origins of which may well lie even earlier than Carn Euny, in the Bronze Age, but it is nevertheless considered to be of later construction. The roughly circular granite structures at Chysauster, whose walls remain standing in a remarkable state of preservation, are thought to have been erected during the first century AD. They were probably inhabited for just 400 years – a period of time roughly coinciding with the Roman occupation of Britain. Expert opinion is divided as to whether these buildings actually predate the invasion of AD 43, and any suggestion that Roman influence can be traced in matters of plan and construction is hotly debated.

A planned settlement

There are compelling reasons suggesting that Chysauster was a planned settlement. Its regularity of layout and standardized house forms, with their associated garden terraces, suggest a forethought not evident in the seemingly haphazard arrangement of dwellings at Carn Euny. Both settlements were likely built by the Dumnonii, a group of small tribes that, at the time, occupied the southwestern peninsula of England, in a landscape that probably differed little from the one we see today. Differences in scale or organization notwith-

standing, the two villages share many characteristics with other contemporary settlements in the region, not least of which are the unusual compartmented dwellings known locally as 'courtyard houses' – a form peculiar to the west of Cornwall (although similar structures from the same period have been found elsewhere in the uplands of Britain). Another common feature of the stone-walled villages of Cornwall's uplands is that they are nearly always close to an Iron Age hillfort; it is impossible to discount the possibility of some form of association, be it political, economic or social. Chysauster, for example, is just 1.6km (1 mile) to the west of Castle-an-Dinas, one of the largest and best-preserved Iron Age hillforts in Cornwall.

Now reduced to little more than two rows of four pairs of houses, together with a ninth dwelling a short distance away and traces of nearly a dozen roundhouses, the village may once have been far larger than its visible remains suggest. Some 140m (150 yards) or so from the nearest house, towards the site's southeastern boundary, the collapsed remains of a 'fogou' can be seen. Fogous (from an old Cornish word meaning 'cave') were underground structures that

may have been used for cool storage, although it has been suggested that they could just as easily have been places of refuge or sites of ritualistic or religious significance. It is possible that the fogou at Chysauster relates to the elusive Iron Age phase of the site, and at one point it probably stood within the settlement itself, as is usually the case with these features. If, as one mid-19th-century document suggests, much of the village has been removed, we may be looking at all that remains of a small town contained within a roughly circular earthwork, rather than a simple hamlet.

The fine examples of fogous at Carn Euny and Halliggye are open to the public, but the one at Chysauster has yet to be excavated and, due to its ruinous state, it is fenced off with steel railings. Stone-lined and covered with vast capstones, it runs uphill for about 15m (50 feet). Preliminary investigations suggest that its floor lies approximately 1.8m (6 feet) below today's ground level.

Carefully positioned so as to face away from the prevailing southwesterly wind, the main entrance of each dwelling at Chysauster opens into a passageway that

ABOVE
A view into a central courtyard from one of the 'rooms' within the roundhouse.

ABOVE
The inside of a house, with what is possibly a quern stone visible. Many chambers were found to contain similar kinds of domestic items.

holes have been found in almost every substantial chamber – probably for a central timber upright that would have supported the apex of a conical roof of turf or thatch. Water channels covered and lined with stone run through the floors of the houses, perhaps to bring fresh water into the courtyard, or to drain away any excess rainwater. Due to the reasonably consistent repetition of this basic plan from house to house, it has been conjectured that each room may have had a specific use.

The Dumnonii appear to have offered little or no resistance to the Roman invaders, possibly because the area's tin and copper trade had already forged strong links with the continent. Indeed, the occupying army was not required to venture west of the River Tamar for any extended period. Isca (Exeter) became the administrative capital of the region. However, the Cornish Britons were practically self-governed, and their lifestyle did not change much; local metals were certainly exchanged for luxury goods, but the tribespeople do not seem to have adopted the Roman way of life. After the decline of the Iberian tin mines and the increased use of pewter and coinage, tin became a valuable commodity and Cornish 'tin-streamers' prospered as a result. Although only one small piece of tin has been found at Chysauster, it remains likely that the villagers panned the local streams and riverbeds for nuggets of the metal.

leads to a spacious paved courtyard, which may not have been roofed. Along one side of this potentially open central area would have been a curved bay that might well have been at least partially covered, to shelter livestock. The courtyard houses boasted walls up to 5m (14 feet) thick and at least 1.5m (5 feet) tall, so it is interesting to note that the internal doorways are frequently very small. Circular rooms and chambers were built within the thickness of the walls. Some of the smaller spaces could have been used for storage, or, since there is evidence that some may have had stone roofs, they might have had a religious function.

The main living area of each house seems to have been a chamber known as the 'round room', located on the opposite side of the courtyard from the main entrance. Some of these have what look like filled-in back doors in their outside wall. There was usually also a long, narrow chamber known as the 'long room', sometimes with a smaller round room beside it. Stones with socket

Domestic and agricultural life

Various excavations of the site have brought to light an array of commonly found domestic articles, such as spindle whorls and whetstones, although the purposes of a small scattering of slate and a quantity of smooth pale quartz pebbles are less easy to explain. Romano-Cornish pottery from the 2nd and 3rd centuries AD makes up the bulk of the finds, but in 1983, workmen erecting a sign unearthed something very exciting indeed. It was a 2,000-year-old spoon made from an alloy of copper and tin, probably used for opening and eating shellfish, although it may have belonged to the local herbalist and had a medicinal function.

In the fields around Chysauster, villagers once worked the thin, yellowish-brown clay known locally as 'rab', cultivating cereals at the margin where agricultural land gives way to moorland. Successive generations of farmers had gradually cleared the slopes, once forested with oak and hazel, so that by the Roman period, the open landscape was vulnerable to erosion. This perhaps led to the erection of early field boundaries in an attempt to conserve the soil. Due to that soil's acidity, there are no clues as to which species of animals lived in and around the village, but it is likely that livestock was reared for dairy produce and meat.

At around the time that the Romans withdrew from Britain, Chysauster was quietly abandoned, for reasons that will almost certainly never be known. It then appears that the village lay unused until the 19th century, when it became known as Chapels, possibly because it was thought to have been used by Methodist preachers, who are said occasionally to have held meet-

ings there. The settlement's true origins were forgotten until it was 'discovered' by a local antiquary in 1849. Sporadic excavations of the site have taken place since 1874, but it was a large-scale investigation in 1928 that prompted the then-owner to place a large portion of the site in the guardianship of the Office of Works (later the Department of the Environment). Since then, more land has been added to the protected area, and in 1984 Chysauster entered the care of English Heritage.

A sanctuary for wildlife, including a thriving colony of rabbits, the village has in recent years become something of a tourist attraction. Some think the picnic tables and pay booths, facilities for visitors, are an eyesore. Others complain that decades of 'maintenance' have led to walls being rebuilt on 'incorrect alignments', thereby blurring the true archaeological picture. It is safe to say, though, that only careful management and controlled access can safeguard this site for future generations.

ABOVE
Looking across the settlement towards the west, the land beyond continues to be farmed, as it has been for thousands of years.

TREWORTHA
CORNWALL

In 1891 a small group of workmen, directed by the Reverends S. Baring-Gould and A. H. Malan, took their picks and spades to the ruins of an abandoned settlement of unknown date on the north-east edge of Smallacombe Downs, on Bodmin Moor. Although they were not aware of it at the time, they were actually conducting the first sizeable excavation of a deserted medieval village site in England. At the end of a two-year investigation, they had completed one of the earliest archaeological surveys; their subject: Trewortha.

To those early excavators, Trewortha was a mysterious cluster of stone-built structures that occupied the slope between Trewortha Marsh and the East Moor of Bodmin. On the eastern horizon, a glimpse of the high tors of Dartmoor was visible through a dip in the granite landscape, while the nearby Withy Brook rushed along its stony course, breaking the silence. Sturdily constructed from durable local stone, many walls and internal structures have remained at least partially intact, allowing the 19th-century investigators to draw plans and elevations of remarkable detail and clarity once the encroaching undergrowth had been cleared.

A settlement discovered

Baring-Gould noted 'nine rectangular huts – ten if we include one on a mound in the marsh, and there are some two or three hut circles as well'. All of the huts were oriented east to west, and most had doorways that faced south. Baring-Gould also noticed that high banks had been built to the west of the structures, which he concluded were intended to shelter the buildings in bad weather. The excavators took internal and external measurements, recording partitions and hearths. The doorways were low and narrow, with one notable exception. Most of the walls were approximately 1m (3 feet) thick, their inner faces lined with upright slabs of granite. However, some chambers had walls of up to 3m (10 feet) in depth, within which had been constructed deep lockers, beehive-shaped ovens and substantial recesses, often next to the ovens, which Baring-Gould suggested could have been either sleeping accommodation or heated storage spaces.

The largest hut was some 6m (20 feet) wide by 25m (80 feet) in length, and had been divided into four chambers. It was decided that the building was originally about 3m (10 feet) shorter, and that the easternmost end was a later addition. Within this structure was a 6-m (20-feet) long room that Baring-Gould called the 'Council Hall', as a narrow row of stone 'benches' stretched along the length of each wall. He estimated that

one row could have accommodated ten people, while the opposite row ended in a large 'seat' with arms (or 'elbows', as he called them), and could have seated eight on the benches and one or two in the larger chair. He also surmised that the 'cushion stones' could have been removed to provide mangers for livestock. He found no trace of a hearth in that chamber, but acknowledged that it may have been removed.

Outside the huts, Baring-Gould discovered kitchen middens (in which refuse was dumped), paddocks and a sunken track. One of the smaller stone circles within the site appeared to be a double ring construction, and showed evidence of a central hearth. Baring-Gould described a larger circle, measuring about 30m (100 feet) in diameter, as a pen that was divided east to west.

A much more recent assessment of the remains at Trewortha has identified, within an area of more than 120 square metres (1,290 square feet), four rectangular medieval longhouses, along with a number

ABOVE

Settlement at Tressellern, with Trewortha Tor in the background. Finds within the site include coins from the reigns of Edward VI and Queen Mary, and an octagonal cheese-press carved into the granite.

ABOVE
This aerial view shows a settlement of four longhouses. The small fields close to the houses may have been kitchen gardens.

of ancillary buildings of various sizes to the west of a wide street running north-north-west to south-south-east. On the other side of the street is a two-oven corn-drying barn. All the buildings would once have been thatched, perhaps with reeds gathered from the marshland to the east. Garden plots have been found adjacent to the buildings, beyond which stretch fields of ridge and furrow cultivation. The medieval boundary is a corn-ditch, a narrow embanked northern extension of the village street that curves through the fields in a north-westerly direction, and marks the transition from the main area of medieval cultivation and the less used land and moors. It appears that the community at Trewortha engaged in cereal cultivation and animal husbandry. The homes here appear to have been spacious, although we don't know how many people occupied each building. It seems that key items of furniture were commonly made of stone.

Having been largely cleared of its trees in prehistory, the landscape may have been quite open when Trewortha was occupied. Today, the site is enclosed on three sides by managed commercial woodland. Nearby is the Trewortha Farm Centre, where a Bronze Age village of three round houses has been constructed, reflecting the large number of hut circles found in the area.

About 1,000m (1,094 yards) to the north east lies another complex of ruined stone buildings. Covering an area of around 0.5ha (1¼ acres), the southern entrance of this deserted medieval farmstead looks toward the marshland. First mentioned in documents of 1313 as 'Treselern', it later reappears in a lease of 1715, which describes 'the Hall house and the chamber over, with the barn in Tresellyn' in North Hill parish. However, the Ordinance Survey map of 1812-16 merely describes 'ruins' there, and so it seems certain that by the end of the 18th century, the settlement had been deserted.

STOCKLINCH OTTERSEY

SOMERSET

T his settlement's name means 'place on the hill,' and that is where you will find what little remains of the medieval village of Stocklinch Ottersey, lying on the lower slopes of a hill 3km (2 miles) northeast of Ilminster, overlooking the valley of the River Isle. Once, the Ilchester to Taunton road crossed the river at Ilford Bridge, close to the village, before climbing the hill; today's traffic uses the nearby A303.

A parish by the name of Stocklinch exists to this day, and comprises all that remains of the two ancient manors of Stocklinch Magdalen and Stocklinch Ottersey. The former takes its suffix from the saint to whom its church is dedicated, while Ottersey derives from the word 'otricer,' denoting the king's hawker. It was the Otricers who held the manor in the 12th century, and resting on a ledge in the 14th-century south transept of Ottersey's predominantly 13th-century church can be found a single female effigy tomb believed to be that of the wife of William le Ostricer. St Mary's has since become the last resting place of generations of subsequent lords of the manor – first the Jeffrey family, and then the Allens.

While the benefices of the two corresponding ecclesiastical parishes were combined in 1886, it would be another 45 years before the parishes were finally amalgamated, by which time the total population had dropped to 123. This new single administrative unit, nearly 3km (2 miles) long and 0.8km (0.5 miles) wide, climbed from 15m (50 ft) above sea level at Ilford Bridges to a little over 95m (300 ft) at its highest point. It is on these higher slopes that the now isolated church of St Mary's Ottersey can be found, above the barely visible remains of the old medieval village, with only the rectory, Stocklinch Manor, to the south and a few other dwellings for company.

While arable fields occupied the lower slopes, the ground around the village was mainly given over to pasture. Perhaps reflecting their likely origins as a single manor, the two communities seemed to have worked together to operate a medieval field system comprising three main and three minor fields, within which the strips of demesne, glebe, freeholders and tenants from both manors were intermingled.

Middle and East Fields were laid out on the higher ground, where cultivation terraces known as 'lynchets' are still visible today; common land may once have surrounded the older closes around the houses. Further down the hill, West Field occupied the area between the dwellings and the river. It contained a number of unenclosed-

ABOVE
One of the 187 medieval churches dedicated to St Mary, the church of St Mary Magdalen has stood in Stocklinch for over 700 years.

BELOW
Now standing alone on a hillside, St Mary's, Ottersey, once lay at the heart of the village, which spread out to the south.

ABOVE

Underhill farmhouse, Owl Street. Once three, possibly four bays long, the house is of cruck frame construction, with a cross-passage located mid-way between the two crucks.

strips, within which a variety of crops could be grown, including thatching straw, hemp and flax. Beside the river itself were the meadows, while around the houses you would probably have found orchards; many cider-apple trees can still be found in the village today. It seems that the farmers, smallholders and craftsmen of Stocklinch were also part-time cider makers.

It was in the 19th century that a tree-planted parkland was created around Stocklinch Manor, and it is likely that the houses of Stocklinch Ottersey were therefore cleared at this time. A number of surviving 14th- and 15th-century thatched dwellings at Stocklinch Magdalen give us some idea of the possible appearance of medieval Ottersey. There is also a fine surviving example in Ottersey itself in the form of Underhill Farmhouse, reached via the evocatively named Owl Street and Owl Lane, and so close to the manor house that a direct association seems very likely; in fact, it was recorded as part of the Manor farm in the tithe survey of 1839.

It is possible that the larger yeomen's dwellings or farmhouses were built under the stewardship of the trustees of Robert Veel's almshouses in Ilchester, because 120 acres (50 hectares) of the manor of Stocklinch St Magdalen and 40 acres (17 hectares) of Stocklinch Ottersey had formed the principal endowment of that charity since 1426, being transferred to the Burgesses of the Corporation of Ilchester in 1475. The surviving evidence suggests that these buildings were of open-hall plan, supported by cruck frames that rested on plinths of rubble. The walls may have been faced with rubble, but they were more likely to have been of cob construction, with the posts and trusses of the roof resting upon them. None of the humbler peasant cottages have survived, so we must wait until some future excavation of the depopulated site can provide us with some answers.

Today, the site of Stocklinch Ottersey is under private ownership, although public footpaths provide access across the farmland.

IMBER

SALISBURY PLAIN, WILTSHIRE

I t used to be said that Imber was the loneliest village in England. High chalk slopes rose on all sides, providing excellent pasture for the village flocks but blocking neighbouring villages from view. With roads poorly marked and tracks that were difficult to follow in the best of weather, deep snow made communications virtually impossible. Yet seclusion could also have its compensations: deep within its remote wooded fold on the Salisbury Plain, Imber's close-knit, self-sufficient community enjoyed a significant measure of protection from both pestilence and civil unrest.

Salisbury Plain is littered with the relics of early human colonization and, unsurprisingly, Imber's origins are lost in prehistory, but archaeological evidence suggests that the first major settlement on the site dates from the time of the Roman occupation. By Domesday, the township was divided between two landowners: the Abbess of Romsey and Ralph Mortimer, one of King William's men; the two sites were separated by the narrow winterbourne known as Imber Dock, which ran alongside the main east-west Warminster to Lavington road.

Water and the unpredictability of its supply was ever a central issue in the life of the village, its name – probably Saxon – indicating a natural waterhole or watery place associated with someone by the name of Imma. The many springs that feed the Imber Dock

ABOVE
A watercolour painting of St Giles Church from 1807. Though in a precarious state today, at one time this 13th-century church and its Norman predecessor would have been a bastion of the village during difficult times.

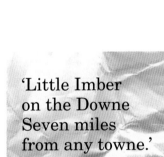

'Little Imber on the Downe Seven miles from any towne.'

LOCAL FOLK POEM

LEFT
Shell-damaged and dangerous, the vicarage at Imber was demolished in 1969.

ABOVE

Tinkers Farm, with its great thatched barn, was one of five farms in the village, the other four being Imber Court, Brown's, Seagrams and Parsonage.

would retreat deep underground during the dry summer months, yet were liable to burst forth with destructive power following a storm or heavy spring thaw. The resulting floods would on occasion sweep through the village, undermining the mud or cob-built walls, causing cottages to collapse and be swept away, sometimes with loss of life.

A further threat to personal safety was brought about by the loneliness of Imber's situation. Wooded hollows and long, indistinct roads, frequently unmarked or merely indicated by piles of chalk or whitewashed stones known as Wiltshire lamps, made travelling particularly hazardous. In the 17th and 18th centuries, highwaymen and footpads took advantage of the terrain by attacking solitary travellers, and cash-laden farmers returning from the markets at Warminster or Devizes would have been unlikely to set out without being armed.

From a population estimated at around 50 in 1086, Imber had grown to accommodate approximately 250 inhabitants in 1377. A high point was reached in 1851 with 440 residents and around 80 buildings, although not all of these would have been dwellings. However, Imber's restricted economy, based entirely on agriculture, meant that the low prices for both wheat and wool, and the

accelerating move to mechanization caused a noticeable drift of labour away from the land and into either the towns or the army, or (for girls) domestic service. By the beginning of the 20th century, there were just 261 inhabitants, and the figure continued to fall.

The Imber of the 1890s was still, as Ella Noyes put it, 'Just one straggling street of old cottages and farmsteads winding along the hollow under the sheltering elms'. Running across the front of these properties, and crossed at intervals by means small bridges of wood or stone was the Imber Dock – sometimes a clear, sparkling stream, on other occasions a weed-filled ditch. Just before the start of the Second World War, Imber, along with its pubs, smithy and church, could also boast an 18th century manor house, an imposing stone-built vicarage, a National School (opened in 1836), a Post Office (opened in 1909) that contained the village's first telephone, a long, cob-built Baptist chapel for the significant number of dissenters in the village, and a timber post-mill high on Chapel Down, where the villagers could take their gleanings to be ground into flour.

A slow but steady decline

It was in 1897 that the Army arrived on Salisbury Plain. The combination of a wide, open landscape and cheap land proved irresistible to the War Office, which had been searching for a suitable training environment, and by 1902 its Salisbury Plain Committee had bought 40,000 acres (16,184 hectares) of land on the eastern side of the plain. Activity in the vicinity of Imber increased dramatically during the course of the First World War, with the residents of Imber being virtually imprisoned in their village at times, and occasional damage being caused by stray shells. But although peacetime saw an inevitable reduction in the military presence on the plain, the scarred landscape could not sustain the local population in the way it once had.

As the crisis in agriculture deepened, Imber's farmers experimented with dairy farming and large-scale vegetable production, but both initiatives failed. In addition, problems with the unreliable water supply to the village continued. As Imber slipped into decline, the peace in Europe grew increasingly fragile, and soon the War Office began to make offers the struggling farmers found it difficult to refuse. One by one, they reluctantly sold up, becoming tenant farmers of the Army. In doing so, they had both surrendered their birthright and relinquished what little control they had left over their own destiny, not to mention that of their tenants.

Slowly but surely, the face of Imber was changing. By the time war broke out again in 1939, many of the thatched cob cottages and their pretty gardens had been demolished by the new landowner to make way for functional brick houses surrounded by barbed-wire fences. Indoor baths and hot and cold running water may have afforded some compensation. But Imber now lay at the heart of Salisbury Plain's western ranges. Despite a scheduled safety zone, accidents were now all too likely, and the question of freedom of movement became an issue once more for the villagers. With the Army no longer able to guarantee their safety, the decision was made by the War Office to invoke a clause in all tenancy agreements allowing for their immediate termination. Imber was to be evacuated.

At a hastily called meeting held in the Imber schoolroom on 1 November 1943, the village's 135 inhabitants were told that

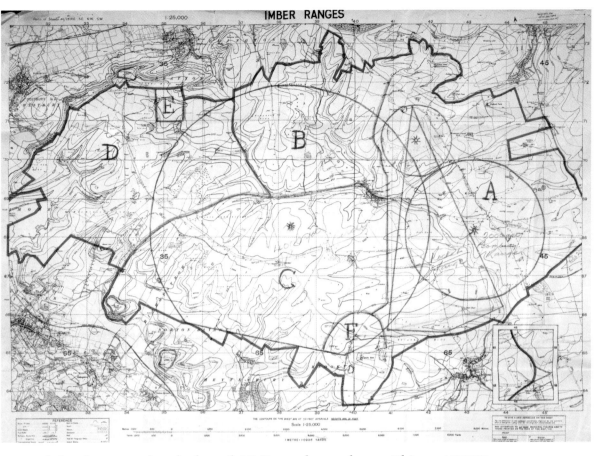

they had until 17 December to leave. This gave them just 47 days to pack up all their possessions and find alternative accommodation. From that point, events follow a pattern familiar in all examples of Second World War military depopulations. New homes were found, livestock and equipment were sold off cheaply and the tearful villagers surrendered their homes for the greater good in expectation of returning at the end of the war. Yet this was not to be. After the war, the government denied having made any promise of return for the villagers. In any case, officials argued, shell-damage, looting and neglect had reduced most properties to a pitiful state. It would be too costly to clear the village of unexploded ordnance and restore it. There were protests, but as the tenancy agreements had been lawfully terminated, there was nothing that the residents of Imber could do.

There is little of old Imber left to see today: 13 of the 27 structures that remain standing were built by the Army, and the village continues to be 'an invaluable resource for training in modern warfare'.

ABOVE
On the above range map, in the centre of the Western Range, isolated Imber lies where two valleys meet.

LOWER DITCHFORD
GLOUCESTERSHIRE

ABOVE

An aerial photograph of the site of Lower (Middle) Ditchford, taken on 8 June 1962.

Gloucestershire is a large county with a varied topography broadly divided between the densely wooded Forest of Dean and the open Cotswolds plateau. Professor Maurice Beresford once wrote that 'the Cotswolds have been remarkably free from depopulation,' a conclusion apparently backed up by the lack of early 16th-century prosecutions against depopulating landlords there. Fifty years on, however, our assessment is now quite different, for the study of aerial photographs and extensive map and ground surveys show that there are, in fact, many deserted medieval settlements in this part of the county.

One particularly interesting cluster of sites can be found alongside the Fosse Way at the border with neighbouring Warwickshire. Upper and Lower Ditchford in Gloucestershire, along with Ditchford Priory village on the other side of the Fosse in Warwickshire, appear to be classic examples of medieval sheep depopulations, the steady drop in cereal productivity indicated by the ever-dwindling amount of tithe-corn paid by the villagers from the early 15th century onwards. By 1575, it would appear that cereal production had ceased altogether, and by 1507–8 the whole area was leased to just two men: William Greville and John Heritage. The latter held Lower Ditchford (or, more properly, Middle Ditchford, as it was known at the time). His rent book shows that he had only one tenant: a solitary shepherd. Documentary evidence goes on to tell us that by 1642, the church at Lower Ditchford was in an advanced state of decay, for it was demolished that year, and the living annexed to the parish of Stretton.

Although Upper Ditchford is more accessible, there being a public footpath running through the site, the Scheduled Ancient Monument of Lower Ditchford is perhaps the most visible and easily interpreted of the group. A deserted medieval settlement aligned north-east to south-west along the west bank of a small watercourse known as the Knee Brook, it has been remarkably well preserved. Its remains stretch for some 300m (985 feet) across a south-

RIGHT

An illustration of a medieval sheep pen from the Luttrell Psalter. Such illustrations have been an invaluable aid to historians in their attempts to reconstruct the medieval rural landscape.

west-facing valley slope. As is so often the case with deserted settlement sites, sheep now wander the sunken roads and raised house-platforms of the old village, their grazing helping the village earthworks to stand out against the picturesque backdrop of the rising valley side. It is an enchanting location, if a little soggy underfoot in places.

The village layout

Popular images of captivating ironstone Cotswold villages do not reflect the reality at Lower Ditchford, where the dozen or so cottages were constructed from timber, perhaps infilled with wattle and daub, of which the effect of the intervening centuries has left no foundations. Even so, the layout of the village can be traced quite easily, especially from the air and seems typical of many such 'clay' sites. A 1-m (3-feet) deep hollow way of varying breadth runs through the village from the south to the northwest, at two points becoming wide enough to accommodate village greens, one of which had an associated pond. Roughly rectangular tofts and crofts lined both sides of this main thoroughfare, while towards the southwest of

the village, a moated site with banks reaching up to 3m (9 feet) high in places may well have been the site of a manor house.

A series of ditched enclosures to the northeast of the main area of occupation was linked to the stream by a wide droveway, and to the east, some large fields alongside the brook may have been seasonal meadows that were perhaps flooded in winter. Further to the northeast, medieval agriculture is indicated by the distinctive pattern of ridge and furrow across the fields. On the opposite bank of the brook, and enclosed on all sides by a wide bank, is a dried-up fishpond measuring 70m (230 feet) by 25m (80 feet). There are also two further house-platforms on this side of the water, close to what appears to be an earlier course of the Knee Brook.

Much work remains to be done in piecing together Lower Ditchford's past. Once a chapelry of Stretton-on-Fosse, Warwickshire, Lower Ditchford now finds itself in the Gloucestershire parish of Blockley, whose history, luckily, is secure in the hands of the excellent Blockley Antiquarian Society. Lower Ditchford has been assessed as a priority site for indefinite conservation.

ABOVE
Lower Ditchford has been misnamed on modern maps. Historically, the settlement was known as Middle Ditchford, lying as it does between Upper Ditchford and Ditchford Priory.

Of this manor Richard holds 2 hides at DITCHFORD, and there he has 1 plough, and 2 villans and 1 bordar and 2 slaves with 1 plough. There are 4 acres of meadow. It was and is worth 30s. Alweard held it and rendered service (for it).

THE DOMESDAY BOOK

UPTON
GLOUCESTERSHIRE

ABOVE
An aerial view of Upton from February 1964.

BELOW
Professor Rahtz's excavations uncovered a Romano-British building, pottery, and Roman or Early Medieval ditches, plus a longhouse, a possible mill mound and fields of ridge and furrow. Highland cattle now graze the site.

In the 1960s, a team from Birmingham University began the second long-term planned excavation of a deserted medieval village site in the country, the first being at Wharram Percy, Yorkshire (see pages 150–151). This second investigation was an ambitious plan, as the excavations were not confined to just one or two houses or tofts (homesteads), but uncovered a substantial part of the village. After nine seasons between 1959 and 1968, traces of around 30 structures had been discovered, and a significant advance had been made in our understanding of the medieval village.

Upton, which is situated in the Parish of Blockley, Gloucestershire, lives up to its name, as it is more than 230m (754 feet) above sea level at its highest point. It is situated around the springhead and upper course of a small stream at the top of a gentle south-east-facing slope. The first historical record of the village appears in a 9th-century charter, although work on the site has revealed evidence of a Romano-British settlement beneath the Saxon remains. In the late 12th century, 11 tenants were recorded as living here; a number that had increased by five just over a century later. The population then began to drop. Even before the Black Death, Upton was down to just four tenants in 1327. Of course, this figure does not take into consideration the size of each individual holding, nor any instances of subletting. However, even allowing for dependents, it is clear that Upton was never very large, and with the lowest tax assessment of any of the Bishop of Worcester's villages in the parish, it does not seem to have been wealthy either. All indications point to the village being completely deserted by 1384.

Enclosed by fields of ridge and furrow, 29 buildings have been identified over the 4.85-hectare (12-acre) site. The buildings sit within 12 contiguous walled or embanked enclosures, many of which appear to contain up to half a dozen smaller enclosures. A medieval sheepcote, where flocks of sheep would have been overwintered, has been located on the south-east edge of the site. The excavations also revealed timber buildings, ditches, stone walls, lynchets, a keyhole and a Henry III coin, not to mention the lower courses of a particularly impressive medieval longhouse. Oddly, no clear hollow-way has been identified, although presumably at least one existed, probably running through the centre of the village.

The key discovery at Upton was undoubtedly the fine 13th-century longhouse. With opposing entrances terraced into the hillside, it was characteristically divided into two parts. The upper section contained a hearth and bread oven, with another structure above it which must have been reached by ladder and may have been used for sleeping. At the other end of the building were a series of pen-like sub-divisions and stone-lined channels or drains. These were probably workshops for processes such as fulling (processing cloth) or

tanning. Sanitation was catered for with a cesspit 2m (6 feet) deep. The discovery of a baby's skeleton buried beneath the floor of the lower room caused the biggest stir, as it was the first known example of a human burial within a medieval house.

A protracted affair

As with the vast majority of deserted medieval village sites, the reasons suggested for its abandonment at Upton are largely the work of informed deduction. All ten of the Bishop of Worcester's demesne holdings were eventually deserted, but unlike Lower (or Middle) Ditchford (see pages 46–47), another of the Bishop of Worcester's manors where abrupt depopulation seems to have taken place, the end for Upton seems to have been a rather protracted affair. It seems that as England's population declined during the second half of the 14th century,

the bishop found it more and more difficult to find tenants for his arable land. The village does appear in the tax records of 1383–84, although only because the bishop paid Upton's quota. This may have been because the villagers were too poor, but more likely it was because they had all moved away. Tenure at Upton had largely been of the customary variety, which looked even more unattractive once the Black Death had created a glut of land and a dearth of labour. Migration from less attractive subsidiary settlements such as Upton, which suffered from restricted pasture and lack of access to markets, soon became commonplace. One by one, the tenants drifted away, searching for better opportunities elsewhere, with no one to take their place but the sheep. These days, the poignant and fascinating remains of the deserted medieval village of Upton are protected under permanent pasture.

ABOVE
It is difficult to tell from the gently rolling village earthworks that in 1299, Upton had 16 tenants, mostly yard-landers. Now, their longhouses and small-holdings lie buried beneath permanent pasture.

THE SOUTH AND SOUTH EAST

Isolated church ruins on Romney Marsh may once have been the favoured meeting places for south-coast smugglers, but did they also serve the congregations of the lost villages of the marsh? And was Exceat, in the Cuckmere Valley of East Sussex, once the reputed naval base of Alfred the Great, really destroyed by marauding Frenchmen? There are certainly many mysteries concerning the villages along the south coast, although less romantic causes for depopulation can also be found, such as the silting of estuaries and the retreat of the sea, stranding many once-busy coastal villages several miles inland.

In Essex, the fragmented and scattered settlement pattern has resulted in a poorly understood history of depopulation. Elsewhere, however, the records of eviction stretch back a millennium – the creation of the New Forest is a story that has been retold frequently. A drop in maritime trade is said to have resulted in the 16th-century decline of the already troubled Isle of Wight, while Buckinghamshire rates as one of the counties worst affected by depopulation, with more than 80 lost village sites so far identified.

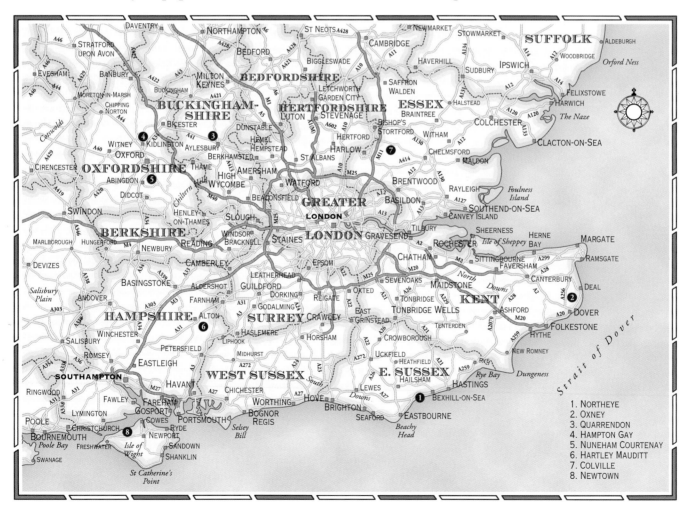

1. NORTHEYE
2. OXNEY
3. QUARRENDON
4. HAMPTON GAY
5. NUNEHAM COURTENAY
6. HARTLEY MAUDITT
7. COLVILLE
8. NEWTOWN

NORTHEYE
EAST SUSSEX

ABOVE
Wetland on the edge of the village site.

PREVIOUS PAGES
The ruined manor house at Hampton Gay, Oxfordshire. Was it destroyed by fire, or a curse?

For a coastline rich in legend and folklore, it is hardly surprising that there are many tales of lost towns that have fallen victim to the destructive power of the sea. The origins of many of these stories may be found in the disappearance of medieval settlements depopulated by the eroding action of the waves or the deposition of silt, which choked many a river mouth. While little or no trace of the settlements lost to erosion will ever be found, those villages stranded in marshes offer a better chance that physical evidence of their existence will be discovered.

On the outskirts of Bexhill-on-Sea, approximately midway between the town of Hooe and the seaside village of Normans Bay, an isolated mound of Wadhurst clay known as Hooe Level rises 5m (16 feet) above the alluvium of the drained marshland. Known locally as Chapel Field, a site on the level has been identified as the location of the deserted medieval village of Northeye. In Saxon times, when it is likely the settlement was first founded, the sea level was higher – or possibly the land was lower – meaning that this slight mound would have been an island, at high tide at least, and hence the name North Eye (or Isle). To the south, and much nearer to the present coastline, a similar low hill called Rockhouse Bank was previously known as Southeye.

Despite the fact that the manor of Northeye has a documented history that stretches from

1188 to 1828, relatively little is known about the settlement. Scholars have traced the descent of the manor, which was variously known as Nordeia, Northie and Nordy, from the reign of Henry I (1068–1135), when Ingelgram de Northeye was the lord there. As early as 1229, the manor of Northeye had the distinction of becoming a 'limb' or 'Contributory Manor of the Cinque Ports' (a confederation of the south coast ports of Hastings, Romney, Hythe, Dover and Sandwich), although there is no evidence that Northeye was ever a port itself. That same year it became the 'liberty of Northeye', with all the associated privileges such a designation brought with it, although later it was renamed and given the somewhat less romantic title of 'liberty of the sluice' due to its proximity to the main drainage outlet of the marsh. However, this later incarnation of the property made it possible to cross-reference an 18th-century list of field-names, with the extent of the manor shown on an early 19th-century map and a modern map of the present field system. This allowed the site of the manor and medieval village of Northeye to be identified positively for

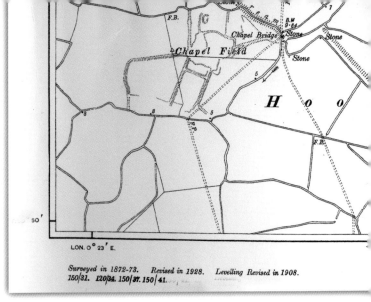

ABOVE
Ordinance Survey map dated 1931 showing the location of Chapel Field.

the first time after many years of confusion.

Discovery and loss

The first excavation of the site was undertaken in 1938–39 by pupils from Normandale School. On the highest point of Chapel Field they discovered walls, parts of a column, carved stones and sections of a mullioned window, along with 'a Roman horseshoe, bones, pottery, oyster shells, roofing tiles and slate'. When the Second World War broke out, the school was evacuated and the project abandoned, although a school magazine report suggested that the excavation had unearthed the remains of St James' Chapel, first mentioned in documents of 1262. Sadly, the results of this first dig were lost during the war.

Just why Northeye was depopulated is unclear, but the reason is probably related to changes in the surrounding marshes, which likely altered the village's agricultural economy. It is clear, however, that it was an unoccupied manor in the 17th and 18th centuries.

From the air, one can see the typical earthworks of a medieval village: the hollow-ways, former streets, building sites, rectangular foundations and small enclosures, low banks and shallow ditches. When archaeologists returned in 1952, under the direction of Mr W. C. Wynne-Woodhouse, the chapel site was targeted again. Subsequently a plan was drawn up showing a buttressed rectangular building 16.75m (55 feet) long and 7.6m (25 feet) wide, orientated almost exactly east–west along its major axis, and constructed of the local clay-ironstone. A model of the remains of this structure was made by Wynne-Woodhouse and presented to Bexhill Museum, along with the finds from the excavation. However, until further excavation of the site is correlated with thorough documentary research, there remains much about the deserted medieval village of Northeye still to be discovered.

LEFT
A view across Hooe Level towards Chapel Field.

OXNEY
KENT

Oxney Bottom is said to be one of the strangest places in England. Ghostly tales abound of a spectral grey lady who has terrified lone travellers here for generations. Sceptics maintain that she is nothing more than a very naturally formed patch of mist, but devotees of the supernatural have come up with yet another explanation, theorizing that the apparition could be the ghost of one of the white-robed Premonstratensian canons from Langdon Abbey who once visited Oxney in order to perform services at St Nicholas' Church, the ruins of which are now almost hidden in the undergrowth of the nearby woodland. During the reign of Henry VIII (1491–1547), an inspection by the King's Commissioners resulted in allegations that the canons of Langdon were ignorant, behaved immorally and that the abbot kept a mistress! The abbey was dissolved in 1535.

A phantom village
Whether the dissolute lifestyle of one particular member of that religious community has condemned him to an eternity of wandering the lane that leads to the gates of Oxney Court is open to speculation. Just as odd is the elusiveness of Oxney village, the existence of which was first proposed by Professor Beresford in the 1960s. In fact, some have voiced suspicions that the long-held belief in a village at Oxney Bottom may have been an erroneous assumption. Yet an isolated church, a manor house and an ecclesiastical parish all seemed to provide valid reasons to think that a settlement once existed there. They are certainly sound enough clues for the hunter of abandoned villages to at least take a closer interest in the locality.

Initially, it was thought that the dwellings of the deserted village had been clustered around the church, although this theory looks less likely when the densely wooded nature of the location is considered, particularly as this feature of the local topography is said to be many centuries old. Archaeological surveys have revealed that the whole area is littered with crop marks, and a number or circular features interpreted as ring ditches have been found. But it has long been known that this area was populated in both ancient times and modern, and these traces of past ceremonial and agricultural landscape have not brought us any closer to an Oxney village.

An isolated church does not necessarily lead us to the site of a deserted settlement. Many such buildings were seigniorial chapels, associated with an ancient manorial estate and its manor house or castle complex. The proximity of Oxney Court might lead one to suspect this was the case here, except further investigation tells us that the recently restored Oxney Court is a late-Victorian conversion of a 16th-century rectory. What now needs to be ascertained is whether the rectory was a conversion, or whether it was built upon the site of an older manor house.

The local topography and the patterns of neighbouring settlements can help pinpoint the true nature of Oxney. Nearby Ringwould is built on a hill, as were many settlements in these parts, both as a defensive precaution against coastal raids and to isolate them from the dampness of the low ground. With this in mind, a recent theory places the medieval village on a hill on the landward side of the Dover Road, about 400m (¼ mile) away from the church.

Documentary references to the parish of Oxney are, however, largely confined to the mid-19th century, and do not suggest any kind of concentrated settlement that could be described as a village. In the 1960s the parish of Oxney was combined with that of Ringwould, an amalgamation that took place on the condition that the parishioners of the latter would not have to pay for the upkeep of the ruined St Nicholas' Church.

For now, the mystery of the rumoured medieval village of Oxney endures, yet it is still unclear whether it can accurately be termed a lost village, for today doubt has been cast on the idea that it ever existed.

QUARRENDON
BUCKINGHAMSHIRE

'Its situation is low and humid, the soil is a deep stiff dark blue clay with veins of gravel and course red sand, and, with the exception of a very few acres, the parish contains the finest grazing land in the county.'

HISTORY AND TOPOGRAPHY OF BUCKINGHAMSHIRE, BY JAMES JOSEPH SHEAHAN, 1862

Hidden away behind a housing estate on the outskirts of Aylesbury lies a site described by English Heritage as 'an exceptional archaeological complex of national importance'. It contains earthwork remains that were once thought to belong to three deserted medieval villages, although it has also been suggested that they may have represented a single village that migrated twice. However, more recent surveys of the area have prompted archaeologists to revise all previous interpretations of the medieval landscape at Quarrendon – and the conclusions they reached have challenged the accepted pattern of settlement for the county.

The name of Quarrendon (variously spelled as Querendune, Querdone and Quarndon) is thought to derive from the Old English '*cweorn ∂un*', meaning 'mill-hill'. When Henry VIII's topographer, John Leland (1506–52), visited the area, he noted 'the Well of St. Osythe, betwyxte Æilesbyry and Querendune'. However, despite possible links with the location of a documented *villa regalis*, Quarrendon never rose to any real importance, and was always regarded as part of the parish of Aylesbury.

Assessed at 10 hides in 1086, it was at that time held of the king (William I, 1027–87) by Geoffrey de Mandeville, but there is no evidence of any great manorial residence there for most of the medieval period. Even so, the manor of Quarrendon was certainly prized in medieval times, no doubt due to the site's reputation as the best grazing land in Buckinghamshire. In 1276, the Crown granted a license permitting John Fitzjohn of Whaddon to create a park there, but if it ever came into existence its location is a mystery.

Having passed from the Fitzjohn family to the Beauchamps in 1397, the manor of Quarrendon was granted to Thomas Mowbray, Duke of Norfolk (1366–99) on the attainder of Thomas Beauchamp, Earl of Warwick (1315–1401). However, Mowbray's own attainder quickly put the manor back in the hands of the Crown. From the 1430s onward, the Lees of Warwick leased and farmed the land. Under the supervision of Benedict Lee, Quarrendon completed the transition from demesne and arable farming to a system of consolidated grazing, with the emphasis on the production of vast numbers of fleeces for the coarse cloth manufacturers. It is in Lee's will of 1476 that we find the first mention of a substantial residential property there: a 'placea', possibly a large farm.

Unearthing Quarrendon

But what of the village – or villages – of Quarrendon? There are certainly three well-defined sets of earthwork remains that clearly show an organized matrix of hollow-ways, greens, ponds, closes, crofts and building platforms. In a county known for its high proportion of nucleated settlements, the explanation that they represent three deserted villages seems plausible. Yet a field survey undertaken by the Royal Commission of Historical Monuments in England (RCHME) on behalf of English Heritage argues for a radical reappraisal. Their interpretation of the site is that the remains represent small groups of farmsteads 'loosely organized around irregular greens' with a 'scatter of individual farmsteads'. This demands that the pattern of settlement at Quarrendon be re-classified as 'dispersed', in contrast with the prevailing pattern in the surrounding area.

As none of the earthwork groupings are identified by name, they have been labelled

Quarrendon I, II and III. Quarrendon I is the largest, covering about 10 hectares (25 acres) of a slope to the east of the site, and is the best preserved. A central green has been identified, with four distinct hollow-ways radiating from its corners; in the middle of the green are the remains of a pond and possibly a mill, while around its edges sit a handful of fairly complex farmsteads, the largest of which occupies the most prominent position beside the hollow-way that leads to the church. An associated sequence of terraced plots may be evidence of a garden, leading to speculation that this may be Benedict Lee's 'placea'.

Situated to the west, across the stream that runs down through the site to the River Thame, Quarrendon II is less easy to interpret, as its remains have been damaged by ploughing, field drains and access ways. However, a framework of hollow-ways, tracks and enclosures can still be traced, which are roughly aligned about a central

triangular green area; a few possible building platforms have also been identified. Then, in 1977, field investigations at Quarrendon III identified yet another street pattern, with enclosures, possible building sites or house platforms and a partial moat.

It is not possible to say whether all of the homesteads were occupied simultaneously. Moreover, as with all dispersed settlements, it is almost impossible to gain an accurate count of the number of inhabitants from documentary sources. About 30 people were judged liable to pay a tax called the Lay Subsidy in 1332, although relief of 62.5 percent in 1341 shows that pestilence had taken its toll. The settlement appears to have rallied in the mid 15th century, when its relief was just 13 percent. But by 1563, the bishop's returns indicate that only four families remained at the site.

It has been concluded that at least one, if not all, of the Quarrendon settlements had been abandoned by the time Sir Henry

ABOVE
The last remnants of the old St Peter's church. In its derelict state, the church was once used to prop up pigsties, and moulded stones from its fabric have been found in the footings of local buildings.

(1530–1610) built a magnificent country house there in the late 16th century. This structure replaced the moated residence constructed when his grandfather, Sir Robert Lee, was granted the manor on a permanent basis in 1512. The 13th-century chapel of St Peter and its churchyard were incorporated into the extensive and elaborate formal gardens, and it is possible that a large rectangular building platform on the southern edge of the churchyard might correspond to a row of almshouses or 'hospitall' mentioned in Sir Henry's epitaph.

After Sir Henry's death, the house was never again a primary residence. It was partly demolished in 1666, and still further in 1713 when Henry Lee agreed to let the incumbent grazier, Benjamin How, remove part of it to build a new dwelling. The remainder served as the tenanted Church Farm. When the last male heir of the Lees of Quarrendon died, the manor was sold to James Dupré in 1802, but it was said at the time that the 'ancient seat of the Lees at Quarrendon' had been pulled down in the early 18th century. The chapel of St Peter survived a little longer. It was reported as intact in 1704, but it had been reduced to a ruin by the middle of the 19th century.

On the advice of the RCHME surveyors, it would be 'awkward but not impossible' to call the three abandoned settlements at Quarrendon deserted medieval villages, yet the network of hollow-ways connecting them, as well as the fields, pastures, meadows, river and the church show that, although undoubtedly small, they had once been active communities. It was the Lee family's policy of engrossment and conversion to pasture that surely became the overriding factor in the depopulation of the site. In 1798, the *Posse Comitatus* (a listing of all the men who might be called upon to defend an area) recorded just 12 men between the ages of 16 and 60 at Quarrendon.

It is somewhat ironic that a place with such strong connections to St Oswyth, generally though of as the patron saint of women who have lost their keys, should end up in need of none.

BELOW
The earthwork remains of Sir Henry Lee's impressive 16th-century country house. The house once featured a landscaped garden with extensive water features.

HAMPTON GAY
OXFORDSHIRE

East of Shipton, on the banks of the River Cherwell, lies the deserted village of Hampton Gay. Now a mere hamlet, it is a settlement whose documented origins lie in Saxon times. It has known depopulation twice in its long history: turmoil and tragedy punctuated the community's decline until all that remains intact is an isolated church, a large farm complex and an attractive row of stone cottages – all of which are likely to postdate the medieval occupation. Only the romantic ruins of the Elizabethan manor house have witnessed more than four and a half centuries of the village's wildly fluctuating fortunes.

'Hampton' can probably be traced back to 'hamtun', which in Old English denoted the location of an estate's home farm, perhaps the focus of the original settlement. By the time of the Domesday Book, with the manor now divided into two estates, there was land enough for three ploughs, although only eight inhabitants were of sufficient importance to be recorded. This later community is likely to have grown up around the church of St Giles, of which first mention is made in 1074. Standing alone amid windswept water meadows, the edifice we see today is the result of a mid-19th century restoration of a late 18th-century building constructed on the site of the original. The suffix 'Gay' comes from the family name of the 12th-century lords of the manor. In 1137, Robert de Gay was the tenant of both Hampton

ABOVE
On the south bank of the River Cherwell stood the old grist mill, which later became a paper mill.

LEFT
Apart from the church, a farm and some scattered cottages, the village of Hampton Gay is now abandoned. Grass grows in the crevices of its crumbling structures, and over mounds where houses once stood.

estates (the other being Hampton Poyle), but by 1219 the de Gays had purchased most of the manor estate and leased it to the monks at Oseney. A year later, as one of several gifts of land to the abbey, Hampton Gay became ecclesiastical property, and so it remained until the dissolution in the 16th century, when the Crown sold it to Leonard Chamberlagne.

Never a large village, Hampton Gay's population in 1279 had increased to as many as 40 inhabitants, shared between ten households. Nothing much seems to have changed until the early 14th century, when the first indications of what would turn out to be a steady decline can be detected. By 1344, the village had been combined with Bletchingdon for tax purposes, and 84 years later it was exempt altogether, there being fewer than ten householders in residence.

We learn from the Oseney Cartulary of 1219 that there was already a manor house with gardens and a dovecote at Hampton Gay. However, in 1544 John Barry acquired the manor estate for the sum of £1,100, and soon a grand new house was constructed on the site. This impressive dwelling, located close to the village, was three storeys high, with a battlemented porch and a bay window on the southern facade. The Barrys later mortgaged, then sold it for £6,400 to Sir Richard Wenman of Caswell, who thus became lord of the manor in 1682. Having passed through various hands in the intervening years, the building was gutted by fire in 1887 and has been in ruins ever since.

Barry had made his money in glove-making, the rest of his land lying in Eynsham, Charlbury and Hanborough, all areas where that trade was an important part of the economy. Already the owner of several mills and large flocks of sheep, he probably accelerated the gradual enclosure and conversion to pasture of the open arable fields around the village – a trend that had been evident since the early 16th century, and which resulted in a corresponding decline in the number of villagers. A similar phenomenon was occurring throughout the northeast corner of Oxfordshire, and in 1596 rioting broke out in the area. Men whose livelihoods were disappearing before their very eyes staged a violent protest against the new hedges and the rich men who, by ordering their planting, had raised the price of corn and effectively appropriated the commons. Armed with pikes and swords, ten men from Hampton Gay marched on Enslow Hill in Bletchingdon. The ringleaders were arrested, taken to London and sentenced to be hanged, drawn and quartered. Though this must have been a huge blow to their community, the men's lives had not been sacrificed in vain, for in 1597 a new Tillage Act ordered that all land enclosed in Oxfordshire since the accession of Queen Elizabeth I in 1558 must go back under the plough.

A brief reinvigoration

The year 1596 has been suggested as the point at which the majority of the village site, visible today only as earthworks in a field directly to the south of the Manor House, was depopulated, although the exact date is uncertain, as is the effect the Tillage Act had on the community. The Petty Constables Returns for Hampton Gay submitted to the Hearth Tax Commissioners in 1662 record ten taxpayers, among whom were Christopher Barry, Mr Edward Belsome, Ladie Fermer and Widor Springall. Three years later, there were just seven taxable properties: the manor house, two substantial farmhouses (one of which was almost certainly the present Manor Farm), a smaller farmhouse with three hearths and three cottages. Yet the village was about to receive an unexpected fillip. In

1681, Vincent Barry leased the watermill to a paper maker, who rebuilt and converted it. As the business of paper-making flourished, the number of inhabitants grew from just 28 adults in 1676 to 86 in 1821, but by then the local paper trade had already begun its inexorable decline. After two disastrous fires, the papermill finally went bankrupt in 1887, the same year in which the manor house was destroyed by fire; in the end, only 30 villagers remained.

Just 13 years earlier, the mill had been drafted into use as a makeshift hospital following one of the worst rail disasters of Victorian times. On Christmas Eve 1874, a Great Western Railway express train full of passengers lost a wheel as it approached the old stone bridge over the Oxford Canal, a short distance to the west of St Giles church. As the driver braked hard, some of the carriages collided, forcing one of them off the track and into the freezing water below. The wounded, dead and dying were taken to the mill, where the storeroom was turned into a temporary mortuary. In all, 32 people lost their lives in the accident, including two children, while a further 64 were injured.

Years afterwards, it was said that a curse had been put on the manor house that day, for it was claimed that its then owners had refused to help rescue the victims of the tragedy or permit them entry to their home.

The railway line still crosses the Oxford Canal at Hampton Gay, but these days the bridge is a modern steel construction and with trains passing at speeds of up to 175 kph (110 mph), people are no longer permitted to cross the tracks. Today, a public footpath leads from a gate by the entrance to Manor Farm across the raised plots and sunken roads of the deserted village, past the crumbling ruins of the manor house and its overgrown formal garden to the door of St Giles church. Despite there having been only 14 parishioners in the village in 1955, and perhaps even fewer today, the church is still beautifully maintained. Within its tidy interior, a painted wall sculpture of Vincent Barry and his family kneeling in prayer commemorates the man who, by introducing the paper-making industry to Hampton Gay in the 17th century, very nearly saved the village from extinction.

ABOVE
The manor house at Hampton Gay was destroyed by a fire in 1887. Locals maintained that this was the direct result of a curse placed on the property after its owners refused to help victims of a terrible railway accident.

OPPOSITE
Disused farm equipment sits rusted and idle in an old Manor Farm building just to the north of the manor house.

NUNEHAM COURTENAY

OXFORDSHIRE

It was long believed that the inspiration for Goldsmith's poem, *The Deserted Village*, was the Irish village of Lissoy, where the poet had spent many years as a boy. While many of the scenes depicted in the work are likely to have drawn on childhood memories, Mrs Mavis Batey, in a 1968 article for *Oxoniensia* (the journal of the Oxford Architectural and Historical Society), makes a pursuasive case for the subject of the poem being in fact Newnham, Oxfordshire.

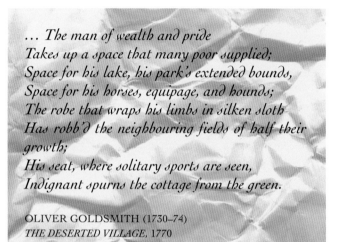

*… The man of wealth and pride
Takes up a space that many poor supplied;
Space for his lake, his park's extended bounds,
Space for his horses, equipage, and hounds;
The robe that wraps his limbs in silken sloth
Has robb'd the neighbouring fields of half their growth;
His seat, where solitary sports are seen,
Indignant spurns the cottage from the green.*

OLIVER GOLDSMITH (1730–74)
THE DESERTED VILLAGE, 1770

A seat of pleasure

The first clues were found in an essay by Goldsmith called 'The Revolution in Low Life', which was published in *Lloyd's Evening Post* in 1762, and is now thought to have been a preparatory sketch for 'The Deserted Village'. Goldsmith described a visit he had made to a village of around 100 houses located '50 miles from town', where he discovered to his dismay that all the villagers were about to be evicted. A London merchant had bought the estate and, with the help of Capability Brown (1716–83), planned a landscaped park, or as Goldsmith described it, 'a seat of pleasure for himself.'

If the town referred to in Goldsmith's essay was London, then a journey of 80km (50 miles) in a north-westerly direction would indeed have brought him to the village of Newnham, just outside Oxford, where work on a new Palladian mansion had been completed in 1760. Built for Simon, 1st Earl of Harcourt (1714–77), the house was situated on the east bank of the River Thames, and on the site of the old village. All the buildings on the slope between the church and river had already been levelled to make way for the gardens. The following year, which was when Goldsmith's essay was set, saw the evacuation and clearance of the main core of dwellings around the village green. No villager was to be made homeless by this act, however, as Lord Harcourt had built replacement properties just outside the perimeter of the park. Here, in the renamed village of Nuneham Courtenay, the estate cottages were spacious and sturdily constructed on a semi-detatched plan of timber and red brick. The following year, it was decided that the now-isolated medieval church should be demolished to make way for a classical temple, the Reverend James Newton, rector of Nuneham, having already removed the gravestones from the churchyard to pave his garden at the new rectory.

Change appears to have been celebrated at Nuneham, for a village fete was held there in June 1761. A decade later, William Whitehead, the poet laureate and a close friend of the Harcourts, wrote:

The careful matrons of the plain
Had left their cots without a sigh
Well pleased to house their little train
In happier mansions warm and dry;

Should we treat his version of events with caution? Whitehead's own poem relates that one old widow had kindly been allowed to remain in her cottage, the rustic dwelling being incorporated into the garden landscape. An entry in the diary of a London bishop who visited Nuneham in August 1800 casts further doubt, relating that the late Lord Harcourt had met with a certain amount of resistance towards his plans to relocate the community, many of the villagers being 'very unwilling to leave their old habitation'; apparently several of the replacement houses had 'remained for a long time uninhabited'. He also confirmed that Lord Harcourt had stated that the episode had indeed been Goldsmith's inspiration.

Perhaps Whitehead was simply trying to stave off some of the criticism that had been leveled at such landlords since the publication of Goldsmith's hit poem the previous year. One outspoken critic was celebrated landscape engineer Humphrey Repton (1752–1818), who was against the fashion, declaring: 'I have, on several occasions, ventured to condemn as false taste that fatal rage for destroying villages or depopulating a country, under the idea of its being necessary to the importance of a mansion.'

Nevertheless, Nuneham Park became one of the most celebrated country houses in the land, inspiring all who visited, including royalty, to wax lyrical on the loveliness of its pleasure grounds and the commodiousness of its setting.

BELOW
Beloved of artists, Nuneham Park has also received many illustrious guests, including royalty: Queen Victoria and Prince Albert spent their honeymoon here.

HARTLEY MAUDITT

HAMPSHIRE

ABOVE
Original medieval tiles are set within later Victorian tiles in the interior of St Leonard's Church.

OPPOSITE
Having lost its village, St Leonard's Church now stands alone beside the village pond.

BELOW
This 17th-century cottage was lucky enough not to have been removed to make way for a landscaped park.

In the Hampshire village of Chilton Candover, a landlord named Fisher, who bought the estate in the late 16th century, was said to be responsible for 'extirpating the inhabitants and pulling down the houses', until 'there remaineth only the church and a farm'. At the picturesque hamlet of Hartley Mauditt, just 19km (12 miles) away, no such indictments survive to explain why this Domesday village should have been reduced to just a 12th-century church and a large village pond.

In a field beside this photogenic pair lie the foundations of the manor house. Once clearly visible as a large depression, with patches of exposed stone foundations and low heaps of building debris, it has now been filled in, the spot marked by a stand of trees. Nearby, the earthworks of the deserted village define the former position of about 10 buildings, associated croft boundaries and other enclosures.

Woodland village

First recorded in the Domesday Book as Herlege, which means 'Hart wood' or 'woodland clearing', the manor was held by one of the country's chief landowners of the time, William Mauditt (also known as Mauduit), from whose name its suffix was derived. Perhaps it was he who ordered work to commence on the Norman manor church of St Leonard, which was built between 1100 and 1125, alongside the manor house in a beautiful forest clearing. There were 27 tenants named, and, according to Professor Maurice Beresford, 'an unspecified number not named', at Hartley Mauditt in 1283. Still a village in 1316, its tax quota of 1334 was just 21 shillings, which indicates that the settlement was largely confined to its forest glade, with perhaps a few scattered farmsteads.

From the Mauditt family, the manor passed through several hands before falling to John of Gaunt (1340–99) and becoming the property of the Duchy of Lancaster. In the late 14th century, it reverted to the Crown. Then, in 1614, Hartley Mauditt was purchased by the Stuarts, and it stayed with them for many generations, as is evidenced by the fine Stuart memorials in the chancel and crypt of St Leonard's Church.

One former Hartley

Mauditt resident, Nicholas Tichborne, suffered a martyr's death at Tyburn in London. A known recusant, he was imprisoned in 1597, when he also gave evidence against members of his family. A year later he was once more at large, and managed to free his brother, Thomas Tichborne, from the Gatehouse at Westminster. Recaptured, Nicholas was finally executed in London on the 24th August, 1601. Was he the same Nicholas Tichborne who, as lord of the manor of Hartley Mauditt, embarked on a comprehensive programme of engrossment, wielding the power of 'custom' to increase his demesne at the expense of the common fields until, by 1591, they effectively ceased to exist?

It is said that in 1798, the then owner of the estate moved to London, but his wife refused to follow him, and so, to force her hand, the furious husband demolished the old manor house. The lady in question did eventually return to her beloved Hartley Mauditt, though, for she is buried in the churchyard of St Leonard's. An alternative account of the ancient mansion's demise is that it was pulled down when the estate passed into the hands of Lord Stowell. Whatever the true story may be, the loss of employment brought about by the destruction of the manor house and park has been put forward as the final depopulating factor that caused the vil-

lage to be abandoned. But it is more likely to have been the creation of that park in the early 18th century that swept away most of the medieval village.

Today, this tiny, scattered hamlet consists merely of the church and its neighbouring pond, together with a handful of old farmsteads. Hartley Park Farm and the Round House, an unusual octagonal brick structure with a conical tiled roof, both date from the 18th century, while the old village street that once stretched from Hartley Pond to Jeffries Farm (a timber-framed 17th-century cottage) is now a minor road.

COLVILLE

ESSEX

ABOVE

A secret pond lies hidden within the earthworks of the Scheduled Ancient Monument of Colville.

BELOW

Possible house-platforms can be seen in a paddock to the east of Colville Hall, while further earthworks are visible to the south.

When searching for deserted settlements in Essex, one is frequently faced with words such as 'supposed', 'alleged', 'suggested' and 'possible'. Some depopulated medieval villages have been definitively located, for example, those at Latchingdon and Little Canfield. But even when the sites about which there is some uncertainty are included, the map of deserted settlements in Essex still looks rather empty.

It turns out that there are some very good reasons for this. The first and perhaps the most fundamental of all concerns our assumptions about what constitutes a village, and our idea of how the modern landscape of town, village and hamlet developed. As Professor Maurice Beresford wrote, 'every English village, whether lost or surviving, represented a community organized for work'. However, the way in which that socio-economic group was physically distributed across the local landscape could vary greatly. In the past, many believed that the hamlets of England were merely the remnants of decayed villages, but today it is understood that they are the legacy of a very early pattern of settlement. Dispersed settlements, or those with multiple areas of focus, predominate in some areas, as do parishes that are shared between two or more settlements of varying size. The smaller hamlets frequently appeared as offshoots of larger villages, and were named 'Ends' or 'Greens'. Essex displays all of these characteristics, and so those settlements that have failed to survive are by their very nature particularly difficult to spot!

The second reason for the dearth of deserted sttlements in Essex is inextricably linked with the first. Settlement morphology is largely dictated by a combination of climatic conditions, the topography of the landscape and the methods found to exploit those two features. In places where pasture farming had always predominated, or where there was a profitable alternative to a dependence on arable cultivation, such as that which existed in heavily wooded areas, the effects of a depopulating landlord who desired a change from corn to sheep will have been slight. Moreover, densely wooded parishes, or those given over primarily to grassland, tended to produce smaller or more scattered settlements due to the less labour intensive nature of their economy. On the whole, medieval Essex had a mixed economy that relied on woodland, crops and animal husbandry. As a result, it was a county that experienced very early enclosure, which again would have dictated the evolution of its settlements. While it is certain that a degree of depopulation or desertion did occur, it can often be quite tricky to locate where the original villages were.

The Uttlesford district of Essex, however, has provided us with a number of possible deserted medieval village sites, some of which are certain. Of these, the deserted medieval village of Colville can be considered one of the most impressive. Colville Hall, in the parish of White Roothing (or Roding), is a well-preserved Tudor manor complex, complete with hall, barn, outbuildings, brewhouse and moat. There is also a formal garden, with a brick gateway dating to the Tudor period. To the south of this structure, beneath a paddock, the shallow depressions and raised platforms of a deserted settlement can be found, along with the remains of two fishponds. There are more village earthworks in another paddock to the east of the hall, while to the north is a millpond and a leat, which leads to the site of a mill that is now obscured by a stand of trees. Little is known about the life and death of this settlement, and only time will tell whether documentary evidence will come to light to offer an explanation. In the meantime, the site is preserved as a Scheduled Ancient Monument.

BELOW
Old farm buildings at Colville Hall, a Tudor moated manor complex associated with the remains of an earlier settlement.

NEWTOWN
ISLE OF WIGHT

ABOVE
The old village pump, located near the road leading down to the quayside.

BELOW
The boardwalk that connects the village with the old harbour area. The salt workings at Newtown Quay have created a saline lagoon that today forms part of a nature reserve.

The five creeks that together make up the Newtown River have been described as a 'watery hand' reaching from the Solent into the north-west corner of the Isle of Wight. Protected from high seas by the serpentine nature of the estuary, this large natural haven was quickly exploited, with several sizable settlements being established along its banks long before the Norman Conquest in 1066. The largest of these was Francheville, later Newtown, which became one of the five most important towns on the island, along with Eremouth (Yarmouth), Sandham (Sandown), Carisbrooke and Brading. Unfortunately, its prosperity as a busy port proved to be a lure for coastal raiders. Along with nearby towns and villages, Francheville is said to have been sacked and almost completely destroyed by the Danes in 1001. Yet instead of returning home with his spoils, Sweyne, the leader of the raiding party is said to have settled on the island, giving his name to the town of Swainston.

The name Francheville meant 'free town', and implies that its citizens were free from the obligation of performing services for the lord of the manor, instead paying rent for their holdings; a precursor to the borough status that settlement would enjoy in the 13th century. New market towns of the 12th and 13th centuries were normally created by powerful landlords

to generate revenue. One as powerful as Aymer de Valanée, Bishop elect of Winchester, who sealed the town's charter as Newtown in 1256, would have had little trouble in erasing any previous habitations in order to impose his will. Newtown was just one of a number of new towns established by the Bishops of Winchester on their lands.

Newtown the boomtown

By the early 14th century, Newtown was a thriving community of around 60 families. In 1344, the borough was assessed at twice the value of nearby Newport, its harbour considered not only the busiest but also the safest on the island. Along the waterfront the quays, jetties and steps would have teemed with life, while merchants and traders set up business in the grid of adjoining streets that went by names such as Gold Street and Silver Street – either a reflection of the town's prosperity, or perhaps an indication of its aspirations. There was a weekly market and an annual fair that went on for three days around the feast of St Mary Magdalene, plus vast saltworks and fruitful fisheries in a stretch of the river known as Clamerkiln Lake. The original plan divided the town land into 73 parcels, called 'burgage plots' which, together with an associated of strip of arable land, could be rented from the borough corporation for an annual sum of one shilling. Governed initially by a reeve or bailiff, by 1365 annual elections were being held to appoint a mayor. A charter under the seal of Edward II (1284–1387) confirmed the town's status.

A fatal raid

But the Isle of Wight was always a target for French plunderers. In 1377, Newtown, no doubt already weakened by the Black Death, was hit by a devastating raid that left much of it in ruins. Other island settlements, including Newport, were also attacked, but while many of them bounced back, it seems that Newtown never fully recovered. It is

BELOW
A footpath follows the route of the once-thriving medieval High Street, now just a grassy track.

ABOVE
Now under the care of the National Trust, the 17th-century Town Hall has been restored and contains an exhibition recalling the exploits of the 'Ferguson Gang', who saved it from dereliction.

mayor and corporation 'maintained a fine standard of municipal dignity, particularly as applied to feasting and banquets'. If, by awarding parliamentary representation the queen had hoped to revitalize the borough, she did not succeed.

Rotten Borough

By 1636, just 12 inhabited buildings remained, along with a decrepit chapel. Nevertheless, the borough continued to hold mayoral elections. Perhaps even more astonishingly, the Town Hall was rebuilt through public subscription in the late 1690s. In the following century, the Barringtons and Worsleys, two prominent families on the island, shared control of Newtown, as between them they owned most of the borough lands, but they did nothing to halt its decline. And yet Newtown continued to send two representatives to parliament. Indeed, George Canning, who became Prime Minister in 1827, was one of its MPs. Newtown later became known as one of the most notorious of the 'Rotten Boroughs', and was disenfranchised by the 1832 Reform Act, when there were just 14 houses and 23 voters remaining. At the same time, the corporation and the office of mayor were abolished, leaving the newly refurbished Town Hall without a function.

There are no ruins at Newtown. Those ancient timber dwellings not burnt by the French have long since rotted away to nothing, while any building stone has been taken to be re-used elsewhere. But the plan of the old town can still be traced on the ground, its rectangular plots divided by grassy tracks on either side of a main street that is little more than a lane these days. Here and there, an old fruit tree suggests domestic occupation, while some of the old burgage plots have survived as small, hedged paddocks – who knows what rich archaeological deposits lie beneath the surface.

Now only a handful of cottages remain, but the old town pump still stands by the side of the road that leads down to the quay. Nearby, its predecessor (a well) can be found in the garden of Old Nobby's Cottage. In 1916, the Newtown Arms closed

possible that lack of capital meant that the harbour was not completely rebuilt. The town's charter was periodically renewed, and the important salt industry continued to be profitable, but by 1559 the market was no longer held, the houses were decaying and an expanding Newport had taken much of Newtown's maritime trade. A combination of neglect and natural causes saw the town's once vibrant harbour begin to silt up until it could no longer accommodate the larger sea-going vessels. Even so, and despite its dwindling population, Elizabeth I (1533–1603) made Newtown into a Parliamentary Borough when she awarded the settlement two of the new parliamentary seats created in 1585. It was said that the

as an inn, to be converted into a private dwelling named Noah's Ark, and the church of St Mary Magdalene (built in 1835) no longer has a vicar, nor a vicarage. Only the Town Hall, which stands alone in a field by the former main street, hints at Newtown's forgone importance. It was rescued from its derelict state in the 1930s by a group known as Ferguson's Gang, who purchased it for £5, and then spent £1,000 on restoration before presenting it to the National Trust. The building is now open to the public, while the Silver Mace, Borough Deeds and seal can be found in Carisbrooke Castle Museum.

During a storm in 1954, an area of farmland known as 'the marsh', which spanned 53 hectares (130 acres), was inundated when the sea wall was breached. Following this catastrophe, the farm failed and the area has now become part of the Newtown Harbour National Nature Reserve. It is difficult to believe that this peaceful 1,680 acres (680 hectares) of estuary and foreshore, extensive mudflats and saltmarsh, with their adjacent meadows and woodland, once operated as a thriving municipal borough and major port, its harbour bristling with the tall masts of a multitude of vessels, and reverberating with the cries of mariners and merchants. Today, Newtown has become a tranquil haven for red squirrels and dormice; wildfowl and waders; rare invertebrates and wild plants.

ABOVE
The site of the medieval quay. Newtown is located on a large natural harbour on the north-west coast of the Isle of Wight.

THE EASTERN COUNTIES

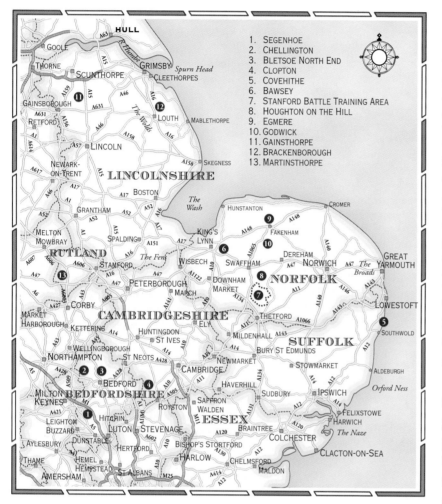

1. SEGENHOE
2. CHELLINGTON
3. BLETSOE NORTH END
4. CLOPTON
5. COVEHITHE
6. BAWSEY
7. STANFORD BATTLE TRAINING AREA
8. HOUGHTON ON THE HILL
9. EGMERE
10. GODWICK
11. GAINSTHORPE
12. BRACKENBOROUGH
13. MARTINSTHORPE

Diversity can be the only theme in a region of such varied topography that embraces low, marshy fenland and lofty chalk wolds, a long, crumbling coastline and vast sandy brecks, dark remnants of clayland forests and the lush green valley of the Ouse. Settlement patterns in Eastern England are ancient; scattered farmsteads and tiny hamlets dot the vast expanses between the large market towns, their outlines advancing and shrinking back, shifting and expiring as climate, community and commerce have dictated.

Such a landscape gave rise to a province of mixed economies, yet this has not afforded complete immunity from depopulation. Here, some villages have slowly starved to death as their common land was enclosed, while others were swallowed by the sea. It is an area that has experienced almost every form of dispossession – the construction of monastic granges, clearance for sheep farming and grand emparkment have all played their roles. Even the modern era has seen villages sacrificed for military reasons, as the future of the nation and more hung in the balance. Yet steadfast resistance to injustice has long matched patriotic sacrifice. Whether it be the Peasants' Revolt of 1381 or Kett's Rebellion of 1549, the ordinary people of East Anglia have struggled to safeguard the future of their communities.

SEGENHOE
BEDFORDSHIRE

ABOVE
A church with Norman origins, the former parish church of All Saints, Segenhoe, is now redundant to all but local sheep.

PREVIOUS PAGE
St Mary's Church, Houghton on the Hill, Norfolk, once served an atypical lost village of the Brecks.

BELOW
Aerial photograph from April 1953. Throughout the medieval period, Segenhoe was the main settlement in the parish.

On the Greensand Ridge of central Bedfordshire, two very different churches face each other across a wide field. One has its origins in the 11th century, and has seen prosperity, pestilence and two civil wars. The other, although built in the style of the 13th century, was constructed in 1850. Although separated by centuries, these apparently dissimilar places of worship are connected by much more than the footpath that stretches across the broad, flat farmland between them.

The old church at Segenhoe is now an enigmatic roofless shell, but it once served a parish and lay at the heart of a small medieval village. Its nave and chancel walls are Norman, but the astonishing variety of local building materials that can be found in its fabric – limestone, clunch, large cobbles, ironstone and cement-rendered brickwork – is testimony to subsequent centuries of alteration, addition and repair.

Land re-allocation
Segenhoe was a Saxon village, and appears in the Domesday Book. According to an early-13th-century survey of the possessions of Dunstable Priory, which held part of the manor there, Segenhoe was the subject of a land swap between the Lords of Wahull and Lee at about the time of the Norman Conquest. Having decided to share between them the fee of Wahull, the Lord of Wahull took two parts and the Lord of Lee, the third. But the Lord of Wahull, unwilling to relinquish 'Segenhoe Park', measured up some land within his allotment, expelled all of the peasants living there and exchanged their furlongs for the eight hides of land at Segenhoe. Such was the power of lordship at that time.

The same survey tells of more measuring, relinquishing and re-allocation of land following the English Civil War of the mid 12th century, however on that occasion at least it appears to have been voluntary. Dunstable's scribe recounts how 'all of the tenants of Segenhoe, namely knights, freemen and all others' who were tenants or held land there 'with common assent before the lords of Wahull and Lee surrendered their lands to be divided under the supervision of the elders'. It appears that during the strife and unrest of the wars, many lands there had been unjustly occupied. It was entrusted to the older members of the community, the keepers of the village's collective memory, who could remember the way things were, to measure and redistribute the strips and furlongs of the open fields fairly.

Shifting the balance
With its core settlement focused around the church and manor house, Segenhoe maintained its dominance as the primary village within its parish for much of the Middle Ages. However, by the 14th century, it was being officially linked with nearby Ridgmont (a settlement that had grown up in the shadow of the Norman castle there), becoming known as 'Segenhoe-cum-Rugemont'. Still retaining top billing, Segenhoe appears to have been the dominant partner at the beginning of the relationship, but gradually, during the 15th and 16th centuries, and for reasons that remain unclear, the balance of power began to shift in Ridgmont's favour. Better communications may have played a part in

this migration, for the road through Ridgmont was turnpiked in 1766. The enclosure map shows that by 1797, Segenhoe as just a small huddle of buildings around the church. By the mid 19th century, even these had been abandoned.

A new church was built at Ridgmont, its tall broach spire clearly visible from the gate of All Saints, Segenhoe. Redundant, with only the manor farm to the north-east as a neighbour, the church has lost its 13th-century slate roof, and was at one point threatened with demolition. Today, it is a Scheduled Ancient Monument in the care of the local council, and has become something of a magnet for paranormal investigators.

BELOW
The orginal Late Saxon core of the settlement at Segenhoe lay around the manor house and church.

CHELLINGTON

BEDFORDSHIRE

While it is often described as the best deserted medieval village site in Bedfordshire, the somewhat fragmentary earthworks of Chellington do not appear that remarkable in themselves. Rather, it is as a key element in the settlement pattern of the wider area that Chellington's value lies.

Situated on clay land, high on the summit of a hill, with breathtaking views of the Ouse valley to the north, the village's low house-platforms, built within their modest crofts, today lie beneath long grass. At the north-western end of the village, the former parish church of St Nicholas, which was built in the 13th century and would once have been at the heart of a living community, now stands isolated in its lonely, elevated position. The building has since found a new role, however, as it is a residential and conference centre for young people.

A multi-parish settlement

From another perspective, Chellington now finds itself occupying the eastern part of the large and relatively new parish of Carlton-cum-Chellington, which was created in 1769. Previously, however, it was the focal point of its own multi-settlement parish, the shared parish being a feature of Bedfordshire ecclesiastical administration. As a consequence, a number of old tracks converged at Chellington, forming a local communications network that would have connected the village with its neighbours both within and outside the parish. From this point, Felmersham could be reached via a hollow-way, and Carlton by a route that has since evolved into a busy modern road; a third track passes westward through the middle of the village site to the church before making its way downhill to the crossing point

RIGHT
The now isolated church of St Nicholas is all that remains of the medieval village of Chellington, once an important parish centre.

of the River Ouse at Harrold Bridge. But perhaps the most interesting route is taken by a hollow-way that disappears beneath Hill Farm, re-emerging in the south east. Flanked by ridge and furrow marks on both sides, this track then climbs for 50m (164 feet), until it enters a deserted settlement site that has been badly damaged by quarrying. From here, another hollow-way sets out in a north-westerly direction towards Lodge Farm, where more earthworks can be found. These last three settlements, all now abandoned, together with approximately half the present village of Carlton once made up the medieval parish of Chellington.

Standing at the edge of the large modern field that contains the earthworks of Chellington village, it is difficult to perceive the overall layout of the settlement; only the hollow-way is clear. Photographed from the air, however, it is interesting to note that evidence of occupation appears to be confined to an area south of the main hollow-way. Ridge and furrow patterns on the north side of the main street may not be contemporary, and it is possible that ploughing has destroyed all traces of building sites there. Conversely, some of the crofts are backed by small, embanked closes that were clearly created out of former plough land.

However, the most striking and tangible relic of Chellington is the church of St Nicholas, the true focal point of the village and the parish. Built largely from local red sandstone and constructed in the Decorative style, its elegant broach spire has been a familiar local landmark for centuries.

Chellington first appears in documentary records in 1242, at around the time its church was being constructed. The village is absent from the Domesday survey, and so its origins remain obscure. A number of Bedfordshire villages sprang up in the late 12th and 13th centuries, Chellington among them. However, it is difficult to learn much about any single village, particularly in areas where multiple settlement parishes predominate, as it was often the parish as a whole that was written about rather than its constituent parts. This makes the pinpointing of a date for the abandonment of Chellington very hard, as, for example, parish population counts were combined, using figures from the four communities.

Local legend offers one explanation for Chellington's desertion, claiming that when pestilence struck the village, its inhabitants simply burnt down their homes and moved into the church for a while before removing to Carlton and starting all over again!

ABOVE
Did the building of the Harrold Bridge across the Great Ouse cause migration of settlement away from the old village centres, marked by the now isolated churches of Chellington and Carlton?

NORTH END, BLETSOE

BEDFORDSHIRE

ABOVE
*A recent aerial photograph
of the earthworks at North
End, Bletsoe.*

BELOW
*The battered remains of
ditches, building platforms
and village streets stretch
across two paddocks to the
south of North End Farm.*

On the road to Risley, 1km (⅔mile) to the north of Bletsoe village, are the earthworks of an intriguing settlement. Situated within two undulating sheep-populated paddocks, the battered grass-covered remnants of up to 11 individual properties lie along the eastern edge of a broad hollow-way that follows roughly the same north–south alignment as the modern highway; a hollow-way that was once the main street of a sizeable medieval settlement known as North End.

It is possible – probable even – that this pattern was echoed on the western side of the road, but that land, now arable, has been extensively ploughed. Archaeological field-walking has produced the only supporting evidence for occupation there in the form of a substantial and significantly concentrated scatter of 12th- to 14th-century pottery sherds. Indeed, the whole site has suffered greatly – extensive ploughing, the excavation of brick pits and drainage ditches, not to mention the modern road that cuts through its centre, have all taken their toll on North End over the centuries. Now reduced to just five properties – North End Farm plus a few thatched cottages – the long process of shrinkage and general depopulation is clearly not yet complete, even though it probably began in the 14th century.

The earthworks and pottery evidence suggest that a planned settlement was laid out here at some point during the 12th century; documentary references pertaining to North End are

scarce. Roughly rectangular building sites, with their closes stretching out behind them, fronted the long main street and were bounded by ditches and scarps. North End was part of a dispersed, multi-settlement parish typical of this part of Bedfordshire, yet its extent suggests that far from being a mere offshoot of Bletsoe or a secondary hamlet, it may have enjoyed much greater prominence. Unfortunately tax returns or population counts were only reported for the parish as a whole, which in the case of North End would also have included Bletsoe village, as well as the smaller settlements of Bourne End to the north, and Whitwick Green to the east.

Tenants and freemen

The Domesday Book is similarly unspecific, recording only that Bletsoe comprised two virtually identical manors of equal size, resources and peasant population, even going so far as to have half-shares in the same mill. The only difference was that the manor held by Hugh de Beauchamp had three sokemen (freemen with their own parcels of land) assigned to it, whereas that held by the Countess Judith had none.

To find two manors so close in composition and extent suggests that an older single manor had been very carefully split in two at some point. However, the situation was soon reversed, as one Osbert de Broilgheld combined the manors in the late 11th century. The four settlements in the area also seem to have shared just the one field system.

An inventory prepared following the enclosure of the parish in the early 17th century recorded the total number of messuages (homesteads) at North End as six, indicating that a large diminution of population had occurred since the early Middle Ages, although no clear cause for the shrinkage of the settlement is forthcoming.

Overlooking the deserted part of the settlement, the large brick barn at North End Farm has recently been converted into holiday accommodation, as the single surviving mixed agricultural enterprise looks to diversify its operations and protect its viability in the midst of poignant and tangible evidence of change and obsolescence.

BELOW
Arable and livestock farming continues at North End Farm to this day. This thatched 17th-century farmhouse stands alongside a barn conversion that is let as holiday accommodation.

DUNWICH AND COVEHITHE
SUFFOLK

Suffolk is not a county that is richly endowed with the easily detectable sites of lost villages. There is reported to be a deserted medieval settlement at Fornham St Genevieve, 3km (2 miles) to the south of Bury St Edmunds, and a broad, ribbon-like settlement with an associated field system is buried beneath the parkland of Ickworth House. But of approximately 50 lost village sites that have been proposed for the county, a mere handful of settlements have left any visible trace that can be seen from the ground. Intensive ploughing of already insubstantial remains (due to the perishable nature of the materials from which many of the peasant dwellings were built) has obscured and obliterated much of the evidence. Nor have the sandy soils, which cover much of the county and stretch into Norfolk, held the shape of any earthworks in a defined manner, as heavy clay soils would have done. Many abandoned villages, such as Wordwell, have been located through the study of crop marks photographed from the air, or through the use of documentary evidence, as was the case at the coastal site of Walberswick.

The town that slipped into the sea

Dunwich is Suffolk's most celebrated example of a once populous settlement succumbing to the forces of nature. And yet all up and down the county's coast, a large number of villages have been lost to the sea. At the time of the Domesday Book, Dunwich was a town of some

RIGHT
Lawsuit from the mid-16th century concerning "a tenement in Covehithe with 5 'manfare' of spirling nets, 2 'manfare' of mackerel nets, and other household goods, sold to all parties jointly by Rose Holmes."

OPPOSITE
The ruins of St Andrew's Church dwarf its tiny thatched successor, built from its fabric and situated within its walls.

ABOVE
*Due to the dwindling
population, and as its
fields fall into the sea, only
a handful of old properties
remain in the coastal
settlement of Covehithe.*

Just to the north of Dunwich is the coastal settlement of Covehithe, not quite a lost village yet, but one that is almost certainly destined to be so within the next century. Clinging to the crumbling clifftop, the village is gradually shrinking back, as the land upon which it was built is steadily being eaten away. Now merely a huddle of half a dozen cottages, Covehithe was once home to a thriving fishing community. Then the parish was known as North Hales, and it had strong ties with Wangford Priory. While never particularly large – its population peaked at around 300 villagers – it could still boast one of the three great churches of the Suffolk coast. A magnificent 15th-century edifice built in the Perpendicular style, the construction of St Andrew's Church was said to have been financed by a wealthy benefactor by the name of William Yarmouth. Sadly, it seems that he neglected to make sufficient provision for its upkeep, as in 1672 the parishioners were granted permission by the church authorities to partly dismantle their burdensome masterpiece and use the materials to build a more practical version within its walls. Though completely out of proportion, the lofty tower of the larger church was retained, and still houses some of the old bells today. When it falls, east coast mariners will lose a landmark that has guided them for centuries.

3,000 people served by six parish churches. In the 12th century it achieved borough status, and its vital harbour swarmed with tall-masted ships. But from the 13th century, ever-stronger sea walls were needed to defend against regular incursions by the waves. It was a single storm in January 1328 that signalled the beginning of the end for this hitherto prosperous town. Hurricane force winds caused enormous waves to pound the King's Holme spit, shifting the shingle so that it blocked the harbour. Ships diverted north to Walberswick, and the resulting loss of trade sealed the fate of Dunwich. Deemed no longer worth defending from the tide, over the centuries that followed the town gradually crumbled into the sea. Today, a small village survives at Dunwich, situated at the edges of the site of this once thriving medieval port. Up until the mid-1980s, bones from the graveyard of All Saints Church could still be seen protruding from the cliff face.

Covehithe is not alone in its plight. Settlements all along the coast of East Anglia are at risk. Even the important medieval port of Aldburgh, 32km (20 miles) to the south of Covehithe, is literally half the town it once was. Its 16th-century Moot Hall, once at the heart of the community, now stands at the head of the shingle beach.

CLOPTON

CAMBRIDGESHIRE

I n 1292, the inhabitants of the flourishing Cambridgeshire village of Clopton celebrated – a licence had been secured from the King that allowed them to hold a weekly Friday Market, and the periodic re-cobbling of the marketplace in the years that followed suggests that trade was good. Even the plague years of the late 1340s, which caused such devastation throughout the rest of the county, reducing the numbers of some communities by up to a half, did not strike Clopton seriously enough to deter the villagers from a major remodelling of their church just a few years later, a phenomenon that was noted in other parishes in the district. On 7 October 1352, the bishop arrived to dedicate the new St Mary's Church.

Yet little remains of the village of Clopton today. So thorough were the stone robbers of the 18th century that it took an archaeological excavation to pinpoint the site of the church and uncover the little cobbled marketplace that had once stood beside it. Indeed, Clopton is a much damaged site. The quarrying of the chalk scarp on the northern edge of the village, coprolite mines in the centre and ploughing to the west, not to mention the activities of the Home Guard during the Second World War, may have destroyed 13 hectares (33 acres) or more of earthworks. Yet Clopton remains not only the finest deserted settlement site in Cambridgeshire, but also the site of greatest national importance.

A village revealed

To stand on the footpath high above the site is a peculiarly moving experience, and not just for the spectacular views it affords over the valley of the River Cam. Yet Clopton is a confusing site, as its component features are terraced into the hillside, and are not immediately read. But having referred to the excellent information board thoughtfully provided for visitors by the local council, it soon becomes clear that the footpath that is used to reach the site was actually the principal medieval through route, one of the two main hollow-ways that served the village. With the aid of an artist's impression, the site of Bury Mount, the most important of the two moated manor houses in the village, becomes apparent. Then the line of the village street, the green and the position of the church and market place, pond and mill gradually reveal themselves, more in the imagination, it must be said, than on the ground. Suddenly, this rather bumpy green hill, with its occasional clump of scrubby trees, becomes the site of a medieval village once more, a place where the triumphs and tragedies of many centuries in the life of a community have been acted out. Stories spring to mind of the poor child drowned in the moat of Bury Mount, and of the villager who stole corn from the priest's barn and then ran instinctively to the church for sanctuary.

All the elements of medieval village life are to be found at Clopton, and therein lies its appeal and significance. Ironically, the reason it disappeared as a living community

ABOVE
The former Clopton High Street, with the site of the church on the left, and of one of the two manor houses on the right.

BELOW
Aerial view of the earthworks at Clopton, April 1974. The deserted village site is situated to the west of Croydon village.

is the reason its remains survive today – Clopton was depopulated to make way for sheep. For once, this is not simply a deduction based on circumstantial evidence and hypothesis, as the death throes of Clopton were documented in court records that make chilling reading today. We learn how the pride and foolishness of one man allowed the avarice of another to destroy a community that could claim roots in the time of the pagan Saxons – perhaps even the Romans before them.

By the summer of 1502, it must have dawned on the hapless William Clopton that he had made yet another terrible mistake. The first had been to live his life in such a way that he had fallen into financial difficulties, but then he had compounded the error by selling his Clopton estate to a London lawyer by the name of John Fisher. Thirteen years earlier, while being pursued by money-lenders, the deal must have looked as attractive as signing away your birthright ever could. William received just £200 for Clopton, although he and his wife, Juliana, were allowed to keep the manor house at Bury Mount, with its closes and orchard, plus a cottage.

William had inherited the estate from his father, Robert, who, having made his fortune as a draper in London (where he had served as sheriff in 1435), had purchased the two Domesday manors of the parish of Clopton – a location whose name he shared, although no direct family connection has yet been established. Although the vast open fields and the ridge and furrow patterns argue for a largely arable economy in the village, the tax quota of 1341 had been paid in wool, so clearly pasture had played an important role. Fisher, however, was determined that Clopton would be one vast sheep walk.

There is some debate as to whether Clopton was actually a village in decline when Fisher began his work of enlarging and rationalizing his demesne strips and converting them to enclosed pasture. A rough population estimate at Domesday indicates that there could have been as many as 90 villagers. Little seems to have changed by 1377, when another very approximate figure of 100 can be calculated, whereas by 1524 only six inhabitants were recorded. Nearly a century and a half lies between these figures, so just what the size and viability of the community was when Fisher purchased the estate remains unknown. However, it seems unlikely that even a man of his apparent arrogance and single-mindedness would have purchased a village where there was not already some indication that he would be able to bring his plans to fruition.

RIGHT
View across the earthworks looking south along the former High Street. Although covered by permanent pasture, some features still reach up to 1m (1 yard) in height.

The best evidence we have for the nature of the depopulation comes from the apparently unresolved cases brought before the Court of Chancery by Fisher, Clopton and two successive rectors of the parish. In 1503, an action by Clopton stalled because the chancellor died. Soon afterward, Clopton later claimed, Fisher, together with the local sheriff, forced his way into the manor house, imprisoned its two occupants and vandalized their possessions. Fisher had already brought a case against the Cloptons with regard to Bury Mount, and it would appear that he had long had his eye on the property. In 1500, a dispute erupted between Fisher and the incumbent of St Mary's Church. The clergyman complained that by buying out and removing the holders of the common arable land and then converting it to pasture – which he then leased to two farmers by the name of Morgan and Brockwell – Fisher had rendered the now isolated area of arable glebe (church land used for agriculture) unworkable. If crops were planted, the farmers' beasts would eat them; if the land was converted to pasture, the lack of hedges would result in the wandering beasts being impounded. From this argument it would seem that the depopulating enclosure had already reached an advanced stage.

Fisher died in 1510, and Clopton followed him to the grave a year later. But the disputes did not end there. The row over the useless glebe continued, with Fisher's son and heir taking over where his father left off. He is even recorded as occupying part of Bury Mount, despite the fact that Clopton's widow, Juliana, was still alive and apparently in residence!

Unsurprisingly, with only a handful of parishioners, the fabric of the church began to decay. An inventory by Edward VI's Commissioners in 1553 found that the bells had been removed and just a single silver chalice remained of the church plate. The last incumbent left the village in 1560, and a year later the benefice was united with that of nearby Croydon, when it was recorded that only two dwellings now remained in the village. A century later, St Mary's Church, Clopton was a tumble-down ruin and the ancient village had all but vanished.

The ditch of the moat which once surrounded William Clopton's 'Bury Mount' manor house, and in which a small child is said to have drowned in the Middle Ages.

BAWSEY
NORFOLK

More than 900 hundred years ago, on the brow of a low Norfolk hill surrounded by the sea, a magnificent Norman church was constructed. Today, the enigmatic ruins of that church still stand, but the waters have long since retreated, and now the hill sits amid rolling green farmland. Isolated churches are often taken as a sign that the site of a deserted medieval village may be found nearby, and for many years now the fields surrounding Church Farm at Bawsey have yielded much additional supporting evidence for human occupation. Yet next to nothing was known about the people who had generated all this material, and so in 1998 the site became the subject of a three-day televised excavation.

A fruitful excavation

Archaeologists participating in the dig were amazed not only by the quantity and quality of the finds unearthed in the vicinity of the ruined church of St James, but also by the range of dates that the artefacts covered. Eventually, it was possible to demonstrate nearly 4,000 years of human activity at the location, beginning in the Bronze Age and continuing through the Iron Age and Roman periods into medieval times; large-scale occupation appears to have ended somewhere around the 12th century however, as no pottery of a later date was found. Tenuous support for this chronology might be found in a local legend which asserts that plague victims were buried at Bawsey in the mid-1300s – not an activity that would have been greeted with approval by local residents, had there been any. Yet we do know that the locality was still in use at that time: throughout the latter half of the 14th century, decorative Bawsey floor tiles, with their distinctive embossed patterns, were being manufactured in a group of medieval tile kilns situated less than 400m (450 yards) from the church.

As might be expected, the ground towards the top of the hill and around the church contained some human remains; unexpectedly, burials apparently continued there until at least 1800. Intriguingly, damage to two adjacent skeletons possibly indicated violent deaths, perhaps the legacy of an encounter with Vikings or some other late-Saxon catastrophe.

It is hard to imagine that this location, now more than 7km (4.5 miles) inland, was once in an exposed coastal position, and therefore vulnerable to Viking raids. As an island, possibly connected to the mainland by a causeway or narrow land bridge but isolated during periods of flood, it would have been a distinctive and unusual feature along this stretch of coastline. From prehistoric times, such landscapes had typically been regarded as natural sites for ritual or sanctuary, while during the Anglo-Saxon period they were favoured locations for the establishment of monastic communities.

First seen in aerial photographs, one particular man-made feature that raised questions during the investigation was a wide, shallow ditch that might have been enhanced by a wooden palisade. Surrounding the church but some distance from it, this enclosure was too insubstantial to have served any defensive purpose, lending further weight to the theory that this could have been an undefended Anglo-Saxon monastic settlement, with the ditch and fence simply representing symbolic boundary markers. Whatever its purpose, it is evident that the religious focus of the site was contained within this enclosure, for it was here that the Norman 'villagers' constructed their imposing church, possibly on the site of an earlier Saxon place of worship. Certainly, Saxon stone grave-markers were reused by the Norman masons at Bawsey for the fabrication of decorative details, there being no natural building stone in the area apart from flint, from which the body of the church was constructed.

Beyond the confines of the ditched enclosure, there are likely to have been dwellings further down the slope, perhaps surrounded by a field system. Large quantities of bone and cockle shells have been unearthed; the latter might have arisen from attempts by local farmers to fertilize their land with kelp or possibly even to lime it using the shells. Perhaps as late as 1250, there may have been wharves or jetties at the water's edge, and, being on a flood plain, the waterlogged ground along the margins may have been reclaimed for agriculture by means of drainage ditches, but at the perpetual risk of it being inundated by particularly high tides, or in stormy weather. Industrial activity in the form of iron-working seems to have been carried on fairly extensively on the north face of the hill, where quantities of charcoal and slag from the smelting process have been found. It therefore seems likely that a substantial number of craftsmen lived among the local community.

Was Bawsey, then, a prosperous village or a monastic settlement? We may never know, but the sheer quantity of Saxon coins and other high-status artefacts recovered here clearly demonstrate importance and wealth in abundance. Oddly, at no point during the excavation was any evidence found of the deserted *medieval* village of Bawsey, depopulated by 1517, and once thought to have surrounded the church, a place of worship that clearly continued to serve a local population long after the Saxo-Norman settlement was abandoned. Only a hollow-way to the west of the church might be said to offer any clue to its location, but for now, that particular village remains lost.

The parish of Bawsey occupies an old yet ever-changing landscape. Less than 1.6km (1 mile) from the ruins of St James lie the remains of St Michael's, another deserted church, already reduced to its gables and side walls by 1845, according to that year's *History, Gazetteer, and Directory of Norfolk*. Once it served the village of Mintlyn, but George Osborne's *Map and Survey* of 1690 shows the settlement already in an advanced state of decay, with only a handful of cottages and the manor house for company. Today, the outskirts of King's Lynn seem to be edging ever closer.

ABOVE
Bawsey church was constructed on a hill that today lies in the midst of rolling farmland, but which once housed an Anglo-Saxon settlement that was surrounded by water.

ABOVE
A milestone at the lost village of Tottington.

STANFORD BATTLE TRAINING AREA
NORFOLK

O n June 18 1942, a meeting was called at Two Acre Meadow in the peaceful Breckland village of Tottington. Dutifully the villagers assembled: tenant farmers and farm workers, trades people, soldiers home on leave and members of the Home Guard. One of the primary landowners in the area, Lord Walsingham, was present, as were several men the villagers did not recognize. Waiting to address them stood a very solemn Lt-General Sir Kenneth Anderson, General Officer Commander-in-Chief, Eastern Command. 'This is the most unpleasant task of my army career', he began, before explaining to the gathering that in order for the training of the Allied troops that had been gathering in Britain since 1940 to be fully effective, a place where they could conduct 'live fire' exercises was urgently required. He regretfully informed them that their homes fell within the area that had been chosen, an area, he added, that was half the size he had been asked to find, however, he realized there were 'limits to what people could be asked to do'.

Some 47,754 hectares (118,000 acres) of land had been requisitioned, of which 6,475 hectares (16,000 acres) were to be converted into a 'battle area'. Within this zone lay four villages and two hamlets, many scattered farmsteads and the homes of 750 people. According to the army's figures, at the village of Stanford 110 people were evacuated; 73 were asked to leave at Buckenham Tofts; at West Tofts 135 inhabitants had to go; at Langford the number was 37 and at Sturston, 27. Tottington was the largest village to be cleared, with a population of 200.

RIGHT
Tottington was the largest of the villages evacuated, yet its once sturdy Norfolk clunch buildings are now little more than raised hummocks in the grass with the occasional recognizable feature, such as this ruined fireplace.

For King and country

Accounts vary as to how much time the villagers were given to relocate. One indignant former resident complained that she had originally been told they had just seven days to get out, but that when it became clear that such a time frame was impossible, a four-week extension was granted. That was fortunate, she remarked, as the villagers had spent most of the first week organizing a petition to be sent to the King.

Promises were made to the effect that the army would to its best to protect homes and churches, and if possible, two weeks would be set aside to allow the farmers to gather whatever crops may have survived the actions of the tanks. In addition, expenses incurred by moving livestock and furniture would be met, but, apart from the value of the standing crops, no compensation was offered at that time (a Stanford Re-settlement scheme was later implemented). This was an enormous worry for Lord Walsingham, who owned no fewer than 14 manors in the area. More than half of the land requisitioned formed part of his Merton Estate where, due to the poor quality of the Breckland soil, many farmers had

not paid rent for much of the previous decade; in fact some, unable to meet the wage bill, had simply vanished. Forced to take more than 1,600 hectares (4,000 acres) in hand, Lord Walsingham had accrued a mortgage of around £40,000 by the time the land was requisitioned.

After the war, when it had been decided that the land was to be retained indefinitely and a compulsory purchase was made by the War Department, landowners were offered just £25 per acre. The price had been fixed at the 1938 value, so that no one should profit from post-war inflation. Tenants were entitled to apply for 'Hardship Payments'.

For most, the financial implications of eviction were secondary to the enormous emotional wrench of leaving homes and villages that many had known intimately since birth; some claimed to be able to trace five centuries of family history within the immediate area. Considering the letters that had been written to Lord Walsingham by the Commander of Home Forces and Sir John Anderson, Lord President of the Council, assuring all concerned that they would be allowed to return when the war was won, it is little wonder that there was considerable

'Imagine a village where your ancestors have lived for generations and most of your neighbours are relatives.'

HILDA PERRY, FORMER TOTTINGTON RESIDENT, *TOTTINGTON: A LOST VILLAGE IN NORFOLK*, 1999

BELOW
Ruins of the Cock Inn, Stanford. The last landlord here was Douglas Baker, who relinquished his tenancy on 7 October 1942.

ABOVE
The small medieval rural church of St Mary's, at West Tofts, was the subject of an extraordinary 19th-century remodelling by the famous Gothic Revivalist architect, August Welby Pugin. The project was financed by the Sutton family of Lynford Hall.

OPPOSITE
The grassy track that passes the churchyard at West Tofts was once the village street, while close by, amid a stand of trees, lie the earthwork remains of a moated manor house.

shock at the news. But these were stoical and patriotic folk who had proved their strength of character when, at the conclusion of the Lt-General's terrible speech, they had given him a generous round of applause.

Breckland history

There are more than 20 deserted village sites in the Breckland. Most had been small and weak, and the depopulating forces had worked slowly. Buckenham Tofts, Langford and Sturston had been largely abandoned in the late 14th century, reaching a state of decline that would qualify them as lost villages; the wartime evacuation figures were made up of the occupants and staff of large country houses, plus the tenants of scattered farms and associated farm workers' cottages.

Apart from the hall and the miller's house, it was said that there was nothing left at Sturston by the 1730s, a state of affairs attributed to the emparking activities of the lord of the manor, Edmund Jermyn, who ordered the demolition of dwellings, ploughed up the old boundaries and enclosed the commons. Jermyn's manor house was reported as extant in 1739. So too was the Church of the Holy Cross, although it was a ruin a century later. By that time Sturston was made up of one large farm and 325 hectares (800 acres) of warren.

Langford, meanwhile, had been reduced to just a manor house and park by the beginning of the 18th century. Its small Norman church has survived, minus its tower, which fell in the 18th century; a simple, mock-Norman bellcote serves as a replacement. At nearby Buckenham Tofts, only 14 people were assessed as liable for tax in 1332, and the village could claim fewer than 10 house holders in 1428; by 1603 just ten adults remained. In the 18th century, a mansion had been built on the site of the church, but all that is left of it today are garden terraces and remnants of the stable block.

Even West Tofts has its hollow-ways and building platforms, firm evidence of abandoned medieval occupation, but whether they indicate contraction or a shifting of the settlement in later centuries is not altogether clear. Close to the church, the old manor house moat is still visible. In the early 16th century, the village seems to have been relatively prosperous. Although Tottington had the largest population in 1942, each village had experienced some measure of decline in the previous century. This was common among agricultural communities, however, and would not likely have proven fatal had the wartime emergency not intervened.

Surveying the grassed-over mounds of collapsed cottages and the low crumbling grids of red-brick mansion walls, it is impossible to tell apart those buildings that perished naturally, when their untended roofs failed to keep out the elements, and those that fell victim to the live fire exercises. Not that it really matters to anyone but the archaeologists, for it has long been acknowledged that there is no prospect of the villages ever being rebuilt and repopulated. Surprisingly, given the continuing strength of feeling and publicity regarding similar situations at places such as Tyneham (see pages 16–17) and Imber (see pages 43–45), there appears to be little or no resentment directed towards the army at the Stanford Battle Training area today.

Stanford is now one of the British Army's busiest training areas. Site access is restricted for safety reasons, although graves in the churchyards can be tended. The churches are well maintained: Langford's little Norman box, Stanford's round Norman tower, Tottington's 14th-century gem and Pugin's Gothic Revival masterpiece at West Tofts are all rigorously cared for. As stewards over a vast and virtually unspoilt area, the army has had to become both farmer and conservator: 14,000 sheep graze the 3,800 hectares (9,500 acres) of heathland, while 1,800 hectares (4,500 acres) of land within the training area are licensed for arable farming. With a diverse landscape that encompasses woodland, lakes, marshes, rivers and streams, the land provides an invaluable refuge for the rare flora and fauna that have been evicted from the countryside by the swathes of dark Forestry Commission pines.

HOUGHTON ON THE HILL

NORFOLK

ABOVE
Restoration work has uncovered a unique sequence of magnificent wall paintings within St Mary's church.

BELOW
An aerial view of the deserted village site taken in April 1960. The village was deserted in the years leading up to the Second World War, and the church finally abandoned during war time.

Houghton on the Hill very nearly disappeared altogether. However, in 1992, while on a ramble with the North Pickenham Women's institute, Gloria Davey almost literally stumbled over the roofless shell of a tiny Saxon church. It was an amazing rediscovery, and one that transformed the lives of Gloria and her husband Bob, just as it would also bring back to life the Church of St Mary, Houghton on the Hill, and, in some small way, the departed community it once served.

Norfolk's Breckland is an area known for its wide skies and open heathland, but although its name suggests marginality – a 'breck' is a temporary field 'broken' from the heath, then allowed to revert once the soil is exhausted – it is a landscape that has been inhabited for many thousands of years, as people learned how to exploit every available resource in a system of decidedly mixed and flexible economies. Even so, it has more than its share of old desertions. Houghton, on the other hand, is a Breckland settlement that was depopulated relatively recently, making the transition first from village to hamlet towards the end of the 19th century before finally being abandoned around the time of the Second World War.

Unlike the famously sandy areas of Breckland, Houghton enjoyed a loamy soil over chalk subsoil, and the local farmers capitalized on this good fortune by planting wheat, barley and turnips over an area of more than 240 hectares (600 acres). As employment, women from the village picked flints from the fields, gathering them in their voluminous aprons. The lane that runs along the side of the churchyard once led to the common, upon which sheep, horses and cows were kept, while around the periphery of the village a loose assemblage of 12 dwellings could be found, with a further nine cottages occupying two nearby fields. There was no village school: children walked the 5km (3 miles) to North Pickenham; before the bridge was built they would have crossed the ford through the River Wissey twice a day.

In the 18th century, there were more than 32 houses situated around the church, but depopulation in favour of sheep is rumoured to have steadily decreased the number, with properties on the estate being allowed to run down. A local trade directory of 1883 tells us that the lord of the manor was one A. Appelwhaite Esq., and that 48 inhabitants of Houghton had been enumerated in the census two years before. Yet when the author Arthur Mee visited St Mary's Church in the late 1930s, he found it stranded upon a bald hill. It was almost derelict, having been damaged in the Great War when a Zeppelin jettisoned its bombs into the churchyard. Even so, the church was still in use. The final pre-restoration service was held there in 1944.

Mee counted just one cottage – although there were in fact two dwellings left in the hamlet at that time, both of which were demolished in 1994 – and a farmhouse one field distant. It was often said that the final depopulation was in large part due to the actions of a previous landlord who, desiring to turn Houghton into part of a gentleman's sporting estate, had knocked out the chimneys to render the cottages uninhabitable.

It is unknown when the land here was first settled, although three barrows have been located in fields to the west of the church. Being so close to the ancient Peddars Way, it is unsurprising that this place, once known as Houghton Town, was settled in Roman times. Tiles from one of the Romano-British buildings are evident in the fabric of the present church.

The village church

With the village of Houghton now reduced to a series of bumps in a field on the north

side of the church, it is interesting to trace the fortunes of its community as reflected in the changes in its place of worship. The first church to be built on this site was probably a simple timber structure, erected some time in the mid-7th century. It was replaced in about AD 800 by a stone building, much of which is still visible in the nave, with its rare keyhole arch and double-splayed windows. There is also evidence of a round Saxon tower and an apsidal chancel. Before the 12th century, the nave was heightened and a south aisle built that was served by two arches cut into the original south wall; their outlines can still be traced, despite being filled in. Another blocked doorway in the north wall, an original feature, derived from the belief that a door should always be kept open during services to let the devil out. In the 13th century, it was filled in on the orders of Pope Innocent III, who declared the idea superstitious. By the early 14th century, the lower two sections of the present tower had been built, with the next stage added about 100 years after that. A steeple was built in 1630, but it blew down in 1665. During the 15th century, the chancel was

extended to 8m (26 feet), and its end squared; by the 1760s it was replaced by the present smaller one. The south aisle was also demolished in the 18th century and a new doorway put into the south wall.

During restoration work on the church, the damaged Victorian plaster was peeled away, and an astonishing discovery was made. Layer by layer, text and images were uncovered, dating from the late 16th century back through time in a sequence that visited the 14th and 13th centuries, until some of the best Saxon wall paintings in western Europe were revealed. Perhaps this magnificent work was completed in the final years before the Norman Conquest, when Houghton formed part of the royal hunting estates of Edward the Confessor (1002–1066).

The future of this wonderful little church seems secure, as it now has Grade I listing. It has been a long labour of love for Bob Davey, and much still remains to be done, with many decisions yet to be made – not the least whether the medieval wall paintings should be sacrificed to reveal the Saxon paintings, or whether the sequence of layers should be left just as it is now.

GODWICK

NORFOLK

ABOVE
What looks like a ruined church tower is actually the remains of an elaborate folly.

Climate change is not a phenomenon unique to the modern industrial era. Large fluctuations in temperature or rainfall are naturally recurring events, the severity and duration of which have always had far-reaching implications for rural communities. The long-term deterioration of weather conditions could prove fatal to a settlement, especially if it was located in an area of marginal or relatively infertile soils, because its survival was inextricably linked with the productivity of the land. On the other hand, it was rare for the desertion of a settlement to have a single cause, and rarer still for it to be immediate. The demise of the medieval village of Godwick – a small and not particularly prosperous community – can be ascribed to several factors. The trend towards wetter conditions in Britain in the 16th century was almost certainly the final straw.

Field-walking by archaeologists has produced some evidence of prehistoric and Roman activity in the area, but it was a small scatter of pottery sherds that led experts to conclude that Godwick became a true village in the early-to-middle Saxon period. In the 13th century, the tithes of its rectory were in the hands of Norwich Cathedral priory, and the

BELOW
The blind windows adorning the west side of the barn were never intended for use.

ABOVE

A photograph of the earth-works at Godwick taken from the air in March 1965. The plan of house-platforms and streets is clear to see.

remaining visible foundations of the village church can be dated to this time. Norfolk was by then an important textile-producing centre, and it is possible that Godwick owed its relative stability in the Middle Ages to the flocks of sheep that grazed its pastures. But it seems likely that the difficulty of cultivating arable crops here was the major factor limiting its growth and wealth.

Built along both sides of a wide main street, medieval Godwick followed an east–west curve. This well-worn route can still be traced on the ground today, as can the boundary banks and ditches of the individual tofts that lined it. At one end of the village, the main street ran beside a dam that retained the pond of a small watermill, while towards its other end, between two subsidiary tracks, lay the church.

Possibly weakened by the successive outbreaks of plague that devastated much of Europe in the 14th century, Godwick's decline was fully apparent nearly a century later when, in 1428, it could boast only 10 inhabited households. Eighty years on, a survey of the village indicated that of 18 properties on the northern side of the main street, 11 were empty; in the fields, the increasing annual rainfall would have made the clay soil progressively stickier and harder to work. To make matters worse, there was a simultaneous fall in demand for wool. With their fields and pastures slowly becoming both unworkable and unprofitable, the remaining villagers must have realised that their struggle was in vain. No doubt those that could moved on.

Godwick Hall

The end for this community may have been hastened by the arrival in 1580 of an eminent lawyer and champion of the common

law, Sir Edward Coke, Attorney General to Elizabeth I, who was later to become James I's Chief Justice of the King's Bench. He bought the estate, and within five years had later built a typically impressive late-Tudor manor house right in the middle of the, by now, seriously decayed village. E-shaped in plan, it was constructed of brick with a splendid two-storey porch, walled yard and formal gardens. The manor house was soon followed by the erection of a vast red brick barn, decorated (on the side that faced the hall) with attractive 'blind' windows that were never intended to be functional. Large enough to accommodate 200 troops during the reign of Charles II, this elaborate building, with its magnificent alternating hammerbeam and queen strut roof, was built across the line of the main village street, implying that by then this route was no longer of any significance. In fact, an estate plan of 1596 shows very clearly that the village of Godwick had by this time all but vanished. The church was illustrated without its tower and to one side of the road the cartographer noted the plots of land that were 'formerly built upon'.

Sir Edward died in 1609 and is buried with his wife, Bridget, in a brick mausoleum in nearby Tittleshall Church. Godwick remained in the hands of the Coke family until the late 19th century. However, the estate was leased out after Thomas Coke, the first Earl of Leicester, built the much grander Holkham Hall, also in Norfolk. One tenant of Godwick in the late 18th century was Dixon Hoste, rector of Godwick and Tittleshall, and father of Sir William Hoste; an admiral under Nelson, Sir William was renowned for winning the Battle of Lissa in 1811. Godwick Hall survived as ruins until 1962, when it was finally cleared away, although the site is still discernible as hummocks in the grass.

Standing on top of this earthwork on a warm day, surrounded by the resident flock of peacefully grazing sheep, it is difficult to picture the misery that an increasingly wet climate and successive failed harvests brought to the people of Godwick. The hollow-ways and house-platforms of the old village can still be discerned. With the help of an interpretive board provided by English Heritage – together with a bit of imagination – it is still possible to meander though the 'streets' of this small medieval village.

The same information board tells us that the evocative ruined church tower is largely the remains of a folly. Built in part from the rubble of the old church, it stands on the site of the original building that had been pulled down in the early 17th century, the folly itself crumbling into its present state in 1981. Intriguingly, it contains some stones dating from Norman times. One theory is that the barn, church tower and possibly other elements of the village may once have formed parts of an architectural landscape now lost to us.

Today, the earthworks of Godwick village are a Scheduled Ancient Monument protected both by law and permanent pasture. Managed under a 'countryside stewardship agreement' between English Heritage and the estate owner, this wonderfully preserved site is one of the few lost villages in the country where visits by the public are actively encouraged.

BELOW
Built over the line of the village street, this large barn does not appear on the town's 1596 map, although it dates from this period.

EGMERE

NORFOLK

ABOVE

A procession of ghostly parishioners in 16th-century dress has been reportedly seen heading for the church at Egmere on misty Sunday mornings.

Everyone enjoys trying to unravel a good mystery. Yet, while becoming adept at reading the grooves and hollows of a deserted village site, or being able to survey a site by eye and judge where the green may once have been, distinguishing a croft from a paddock or tracing the network of hollow-ways and marking the settlement's boundaries are all undoubtedly satisfying, usually they are not enough. For a village is more than just a physical framework, it is a community, and until we can successfully repopulate the remains of our lost villages and understand even a little of the stresses and circumstances that could lead an entire community to abandon their homes, whether abruptly or over time, there will always be a sense of unfinished business.

Perhaps mysteries are only enjoyable when there is real hope of some answers. Unfortunately, the documentary evidence for many deserted settlement sites is such that it is unlikely – although not impossible – that any detailed picture will emerge about what occurred there and why. And so to find three such sites in close proximity is triply frustrating. In his book entitled *Deserted Villages in Norfolk*, Alan Davison has identified an area a short distance to the east of Little Walsingham where a neat triangle of such mysterious village desertions can be found: Egmere, Waterden and Quarles.

A ruined church

Isolated churches are relatively commonplace in East Anglia, and each of these three villages has the ruins of a church in varying stages of preservation, but the physical remains at Egmere are without doubt the most impressive. Now a Scheduled Ancient Monument, the site is split into three distinct areas. At the heart of the old village, located immediately to the south of the present road, was a church and manor house grouping. High on its grassy mound, St Edmund's may have had Saxon origins, but there is little more than the impressive three-stage tower left, and that is almost certainly 14th century, although some Norman features persist in fragments of the nave. The tower stairs are more or less intact, but locals warn that the ruins are in a dangerous state and on no account should anyone venture inside, let alone attempt to climb them! There is a precipitous drop into a large basin-like hollow on the west side of the church, a feature variously described as a dried out pond or a rather large marl pit.

BELOW

A mid-14th century licence granting John le Leche of Egmere permission to enclose a pond in the village.

House and garden

Buried beneath the pasture nearby are the manor house with its associated formal gardens, which date to either the 16th or 17th century. Further west can be found the earthworks of tofts and irregularly sized rectangular building platforms, while to the north, on the other side of the modern road, are what appear to be a sequence of fish ponds. All three areas are joined by a hollow-way that runs southward from the ponds before turning south-westward around the church and on to what may have been the main area of habitation in the west.

The Domesday Commissioners documented a substantial settlement at Egmere when they visited the site in the late 11th century. Despite weathering the Black Death reasonably well, the fact that the village was by then assessed with neighbouring Quarles indicates that all was not entirely well here. Its tax payments fell fairly consistently, and were in the mid-range of what was being paid by other villages in the vicinity. In 1428, Egmere paid no parish tax, as there were fewer than 10 households in the village; the Lay Subsidy contribution of 1449 saw the two settlements granted relief of 40 percent, and by 1524–25 its payment was minimal. Yet this brief chronology of decline is all we know about the abandonment of the former Saxon village of Egmere. Just why failure should have followed so hard on the heels of the construction of the imposing tower of St Edmund's Church is indeed a mystery.

ABOVE
One of the more pronounced earthwork features of the lost village site, this deep basin, located on the west side of the church, has been explained as being either a marl-pit or a dried-up pond.

GAINSTHORPE
LINCOLNSHIRE

ABOVE
In a field beside Gainsthorpe Farm lie the well-preserved earthworks that represent part of the lost medieval village of Gainsthorpe.

In 1697, when Abraham de la Pryme, the Vicar of Broughton, set off on his horse for the 'infamous' town that had once been Gainsthorpe, or Gainstrop as he called it, he seems to have been expecting to find the ruins of 'a pretty large town'. What he discovered when he got there were 'the foundations of about two hundred buildings' and 'three streets very fair'. In time, the legend of the village's supposedly violent end was forgotten, and the foundations of the settlement either disappeared beneath grass or fell foul of the plough.

Despite its entry in the Domesday Book, Gainsthorpe failed to make it onto Canon Foster's 1924 list of lost villages, which was published as an appendix to *The Lincolnshire Domesday and the Lindsey Survey*. By then, its identity in the imagination of the people who

'Tradition says that that town was, in times of yore, exceeding infamous for robberies, and that nobody inhabited there but thieves; and that the country having for a long while endured all their villanies, they at last, when they could suffer them no longer, rose with one consent, and pulled the same down about their ears.'

EXTRACT FROM THE DIARY OF ABRAHAM DE LA PRYME, 1697

lived in the area had changed, as they no longer pictured a den of thieves destroyed by vigilante neighbours, as recounted in de la Pryme's diary. Instead, the sunken lanes, boundary banks and ditches just 500m (1,640 feet) to the west of Ermine Street, the Roman road that linked Lincoln and York, had been transformed into a Roman camp.

Identified from the air

An invitation to photograph the camp from the air led to the first identification of a lost village by this method. In April 1925, the archaeologist and geographer O.G.S Crawford flew over Hilbastow Parish and instantly identified the earthworks below – not as the expected Roman camp, but as a

lost village site. He later recalled reading a description of a deserted medieval village in the 17th-century diary of a Broughton curate, and realized that the village in the photograph must be Gainsthorpe.

Now recognized as one of the most impressive deserted medieval village sites in Lincolnshire, the earthworks of Gainsthorpe have been scheduled as an ancient monument and, in the care of English Heritage, the site has been made accessible to the public. What survives today is only a small fragment of the village that de la Pryme would have seen; although he did eventually lower his estimate from two hundred houses to nearer one hundred. Nor is it likely to represent the core of the settlement, which probably lay a few hundred metres to the north. Even so, what has survived the plough probably represents a manorial complex or courtyard farm, with a fishpond and two dovecotes, as well as about 30 longhouses and outbuildings or barns, plus associated tofts and crofts. Sadly, no trace remains of the windmill and chapel that were recorded in 1208. Interspersed throughout the settlement are areas of ridge and furrow, suggesting a fairly dispersed settlement with as many as six streets. That the two streets identified within the surviving fragment run perpendicular to Ermine Street has led some scholars to see continuity with a pattern of land use established during the Roman period.

It is certain that Gainsthorpe had been completely abandoned some time before 1697. But why? Even de la Pryme did not believe the story of lawlessness and retribution. In fact, his verdict is echoed by historians today: 'I fancy that the town has been eaten up with time, poverty and pasturage'.

ABOVE
An aerial view of Gainsthorpe taken by O.G.S. Crawford in April 1925.

LEFT
The rectangular earthworks at Gainsthorpe tend to represent dwellings and associated buildings, while the circular features are thought to be the remains of dovecotes.

BRACKENBOROUGH
LINCOLNSHIRE

ABOVE
Taken in June 1951, this aerial view shows the extent of the earthworks at Brackenborough, but it cannot convey their depth.

OPPOSITE
In 1495, two sisters inherited pastures in Brackenborough called 'le Est Feldes' and 'le West Feldes' respectively; these were almost certainly the former open fields of the village.

BELOW
This excellent lost village site is protected under permanent pasture.

Even the best photographs of Brackenborough do not do the site justice. The interlocking grid of rectangles appears flat, and the hollow-ways and ditches look shallow. The sheer scale of the undulations on the ground fails to manifest itself in an image that records banks and ditches that are green-on-green. The only way to really appreciate the drama of the site, the exceptional 'sunken-ness' of its dipping streets or the gradient of the steep banks whose heights afford their climbers exceptional views of the surrounding countryside, is to walk among the entombed village remains. Luckily, Brackenborough deserted medieval village is an 'educational access' site under the Countryside Stewardship Scheme, which means that visitors are actively encouraged and organized, with organized Heritage Walks through the site a regular occurrence.

The earthworks of the deserted village of Brackenborough lie roughly to the south, east and north of the moated manor house of Brackenborough Hall, which lies just 4km (2.5 miles) from the town of Louth in the Middle Marsh of Lincolnshire. A spring-line settlement with Saxon origins, the estate was granted to Alfred of Lincoln at the time of the Norman Conquest. Twenty years later, as the Domesday Book was being compiled, Brackenborough was held by Ranulph, 'Alvred's man'. Later, through marriage, the line of inheritance led to the estate becoming part of the Barony of Bayeux, and so it remained until 1514, when in recognition of services rendered at the battle of Flodden, the lands passed to Lord Howard, son of the Duke of Norfolk. The family of de Brakenburgh had been sub-tenants of the estate for many years by the time Robert de Brakenburgh married the Bayeux heiress Joan de Rabayne in the late 13th century, but the connection was severed in 1342 when, following the death of another Robert de Brakenburgh, his widow remarried and her new husband, Thomas de Mussenden, a 'king's yeoman', became lord of the manor.

The terrible century

Throughout the early 14th century, a succession of terrible summers and correspondingly poor harvests coincided with high levels of population growth. Everywhere in the country there was famine and poverty, so that when the Black Death struck in 1347, many people were weak and vulnerable. Although the population of Lincolnshire was reduced by as much as 45 percent, Brackenborough, while no doubt affected, appears to have rallied in the years following the Great Pestilence, and by 1377 had a population of about 44.

While the years of plague had not destroyed the village, they had all but wiped out the way of life upon which its social structure had hitherto been based. As the terrible century drew to a close, the days of free labour and services exchanged for small allotments of land and protection became a thing of the past. Despite desperate attempts by landowners to turn back the tide, change was inevitable. With a smaller population, wage-earning labourers became the norm, land holdings grew larger and the conditions of tenure by which they were held changed, with leasehold agreements becoming increasingly popular. Farmers, often sub-tenants of sub-tenants,

now managed the land. One such famer was John Calyeys of Brackenborough, whose name was mentioned in an enquiry of 1399.

A century later, documents suggest that the great open arable fields of Brackenborough had been turned over to pasture, indicating that by this time, the old way of life in the village was over and depopulation had probably already begun. Although Brackenborough continued to be assessed for tax, its contribution was small in 1497–98; by 1549, Ellyn Clifford of Brackenborough Hall was the only record-ed inhabitant eligible to pay tax, while the Diocesan Return of 1563, despite being required to report on the number of families present in each diocese, does not include Brackenborough at all.

Brackenborough today

The present Brackenborough Hall is a 16th–18th-century moated manor house, which possibly post-dates the village's demise. The platform upon which it is built is exceptionally large, at around 0.8 hectares (2 acres), which may mean that it once supported some form of manor complex. Nearby, the village earthworks are oriented on a northwest–southeast alignment. Air photographs clearly show a layout of rectangular platforms that are sep-arated by banks and ditches of more than a metre in depth. One especially clearly defined hollow-way is interpreted as a 'street', and has been described as leading to a possible market place. No site for a church has yet been identified, although a 1377 document is said to refer the existence of a place of worship here. A full interpreta-tive analysis of the site may be some way off, but the quality of the earthworks surely qualifies Brackenborough as one of the best surviving deserted medieval villages in Lincolnshire.

In Brackenborough (is) 1 bovate of land to the geld. (There is) land for 2 oxen. Ranulph, Alvred's man, has 1 plough there and 4 villans with half a plough. (It is) Sokeland of Alvingham, and (there are) 10 acres of meadow.

THE DOMESDAY BOOK

MARTINSTHORPE
RUTLAND

An information board by a crumbling stone farmhouse marks the location of the lost medieval village of Martinsthorpe. Nearby, the profiles of house-platforms, hollow-ways and even a moated area – possibly the site of an early medieval manor house – are clearly visible beneath the pasture. Detailed surveys of the site have also identified closes, a mineral spring and a pond, along with evidence of ridge and furrow formations, while excavations in the 1960s showed that the 17th-century construction of Martinsthorpe Hall and its associated outbuildings disturbed many of the archaeological remains at the core of the medieval settlement.

Unfortunately, as much as half of the site was lost to the plough before Martinsthorpe achieved protection as a Scheduled Ancient Monument. Nevertheless, much valuable information survives in old aerial photographs, and the Rutland Local History and Record Society has engaged in several seasons of field-walking and metal detecting. Their efforts were rewarded with a large number of discoveries that spanned many centuries, from the Roman period right through to the post-medieval era, providing the first evidence of habitation at Martinsthorpe before the 11th century.

There is no mention of the village in the Domesday Book; the first known documentary reference appears in papers describing a land division of 1199. The name Martinsthorpe is thought to derive from a combination of St Martin, a 5th-century French saint, and 'thorp', a word that probably originated in Scandinavia, and which suggests that the village was an ancillary settlement, perhaps associated with a nearby village such as of Preston or Manton.

In the early part of the 13th century, Martinsthorpe was sub-let to the de Seyton family by the de Montforts, who in turn held the land from the Earl of Warwick. The de Seytons continued as lords of Martinsthorpe until the 15th century, when the site passed through marriage to the Feildings, who later became Earls of Denbigh. Even then, the village was not large. There were just 14 house-holders recorded in 1327, with 39 people paying the poll tax 50 years later. By 1445, it was in receipt of a hefty 50 percent relief on taxes. With a similar allowance made in 1489, the village was clearly in decline.

While we cannot accurately pin-point the exact date of desertion, it seems likely that the main drift of depopulation had occurred by 1522, from which time the land was given over to pasture and meadow. However, a map of the region by the famed cartographer Christopher

Martinsthorp House, on the South Side.

Saxton (1543–1610) suggests that there may still have been buildings at the site in the 1570s. It is almost certain, however, that the village had been mostly, if not completely, abandoned by the time work got underway on the Earl of Denbigh's grand emparked country seat in the early 17th century.

Lost to water

Situated on a ridge between the Rivers Gwash and Chater, Martinsthorpe lay at the intersection of a road that ran southwards from Gunthorpe and an old track, possibly an ancient Bronze Age ridgeway, which ran eastwards through the village from Manton and the Oakham to Uppingham road. There are extensive views over the lowlands to the south from the ridge, and also to the north east, where the scenery is dominated today by the vast silver expanse of Rutland Water reservoir. Completed in 1977, this is one of the largest man-made reservoirs in Europe, covering an area of some 1,250 hectares (3,100 acres), as well as the sites of at least three villages.

Long before flooding commenced, Normanton village had already been cleared to make way for Sir Gilbert Heathcote's fine Palladian mansion, which was built in 1764. It was demolished in 1925, although the church was saved, and is now a museum and a famous Rutland landmark. The buildings of Nether Hambleton and most of Middle Hambleton were demolished in the 1970s, before the settlements were submerged. All that is left of the settlements in this area are the Jacobean 'Old Hall' farm, and the village of Upper Hambleton, now just plain Hambleton, both of which are virtually stranded in the middle of the reservoir.

BELOW
Old Hall farm is the only building remaining at Martinsthorpe. Formerly the stable block of Martinsthorpe House, it was converted into a farmhouse.

CENTRAL ENGLAND AND THE WEST

It was the ineffectiveness of previous attempts by the State to halt depopulating enclosure that prompted Wolsey's Commissions of Inquiry of 1517. Countrywide offences against the statutes of 1489 and later were investigated, but it soon became apparent that some regions had fared better than others. Between them, the counties of Northamptonshire, Warwickshire, Leicestershire and Nottinghamshire accounted for more than 40 percent of the national total of ensuing prosecutions, while Derbyshire produced no returns and Worcestershire was not visited at all. Of course, it could be argued that the Inquiry of 1517 had missed the peak of that agrarian phenomenon, which seems to have occurred in the middle of the 15th century.

Yet even before that time, many settlements had been abandoned. Derbyshire's Peak District is littered with the remains of Romano-British settlements such as that at the enigmatic Chee Tor. Conversely the expansion of towns like Nottingham has seen the repopulation of several places formerly reported as lost.

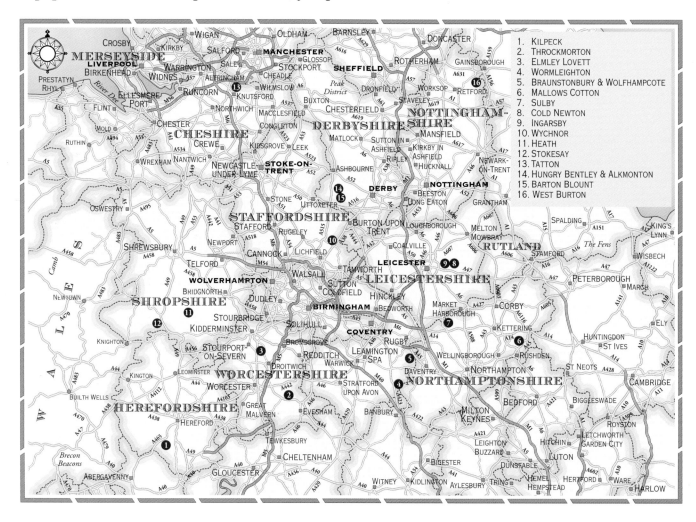

1. KILPECK
2. THROCKMORTON
3. ELMLEY LOVETT
4. WORMLEIGHTON
5. BRAUNSTONBURY & WOLFHAMPCOTE
6. MALLOWS COTTON
7. SULBY
8. COLD NEWTON
9. INGARSBY
10. WYCHNOR
11. HEATH
12. STOKESAY
13. TATTON
14. HUNGRY BENTLEY & ALKMONTON
15. BARTON BLOUNT
16. WEST BURTON

KILPECK
HEREFORDSHIRE

ABOVE
The elaborately carved Norman church of Saints Mary and David.

PREVIOUS PAGES
The cooling towers of West Burton Power Station, Nottinghamshire, overshadow the lost village site there.

BELOW
Immediately west of the church stand the masonry remains of a multi-sided 12th-century keep.

Kilpeck is famous for its small Norman church – and rightly so, for it is a masterpiece of 12th-century sandstone carving. By its side, the mound of a contemporary castle motte also attracts attention. But perhaps it is only those who wander to the far western end of the churchyard to read the information board there who realize that the strangely moated fields on the opposite side of the church actually represent the 2.5-hectare (6-acre) site of a well-defended medieval village.

It is believed that beneath the layers of medieval evidence, the remains of a Saxon village also exist, the origins of which lie in the 8th century. Perhaps the earliest settlement of its kind in Herefordshire, 'Kil Pedic' was an outpost of Saxon settlers on the Mercian side of Offa's Dyke, and it may well have had ditch and palisade defences even then. The first part of the name derives from the Welsh word 'Kil' (or monastic 'cell'), and identifies the ancient site of the hermitage of St Pedic. Situated south of Worm Brook, the village lay in Ergyng, which is today known as Archenfield, and was once a territory of the kings of Gwent. After the Norman Conquest, however, these lands belonged to King William I (1027–1087).

Castle defences

William FitzNorman, the first Lord of Kilpeck, built a motte and bailey castle here; one of 40 such structures in Herefordshire that were intended to protect the English from Welsh attack, plus keep the local population in check. Initially of timber construction, the keep was replaced by a stone structure in about 1190, fragments of which are still visible today. Extending to the

north-east, it seems likely that the castle's extensive rectangular outer defences were constructed over the top of the Saxon village. However, the small 'burgh' sheltering under the protection of this massive Norman keep quickly became the new administrative centre of Archenfield, and the re-established community soon prospered.

Kilpeck has its entry in the Domesday Book under the title of 'Chipeete'. With two serfs, four oxmen, 57 men and a total of 22 ploughs recorded, it was clearly a settlement of some size at this point. Yet the community's Saxon church is not mentioned, possibly because it fell within the Welsh diocese of Llandaff, and so was not liable for English taxes. Llandaff lost its Archenfield parishes to the diocese of Hereford early in the 12th century, shortly before construction started on the present church of St Mary and St David. Apart from the north-east corner of the nave, which seems to be a relic of the earlier Saxon edifice, Kilpeck's new church, adorned with magnificent sandstone carvings, was completed in about 1142.

Surrounded by ancient oak woodland that stretched almost to the foot of the Black Mountains in the west, the castle was at the centre of extensive hunting grounds. It was probably for this reason that King John (1166–1216) paid several visits to Kilpeck in the early 13th century, as the guest of William de Cantilupe, Sheriff of Herefordshire. The village was granted a weekly Friday Market and annual fair in 1244, (confirmed in 1259 and 1309), with the old market place in all likelihood occupying the open space in front of the church. However, as the Welsh Marches became more settled, and the military function of the castle diminished, local demand for goods and services declined. Even before the depredations of the Black Death, neglect from absentee landlords combined with years of famine had greatly diminished the community's wealth.

By 1428, the nearby priory, a small cell of the Benedictine Abbey of Gloucester, was dissolved, having repeatedly lapsed into debt, while the castle was already in ruins by the time Royalist troops established a garrison there during the English Civil War. Even so, it is Cromwell's men who are blamed for the final destruction of the castle upon its eventual capture. Many of its stones can be found in the fabric of Kilpeck Court 30m (100 feet) to the south-east of the church.

As for the village, although classified as 'very good', the earthworks of its deserted site are best seen from the air, where they trace a clearly defined pattern of roads, with crofts lying at right angles to a main north-east to south-west hollow-way that runs through the centre – now used as a modern road through the village. Unfortunately, much of the evidence to the south-east of this old main street has been ploughed out.

Yet however diminished the community at Kilpeck became it did not completely disappear. Visitors to the church will notice that there is clearly still a small village there today. Rather than being completely abandoned, it would seem that the settlement either shrank to its present extent or, over time, migrated to its current position.

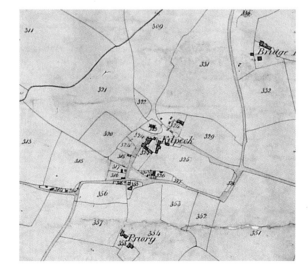

ABOVE
It is said that the masons who built the church at Kilpeck were inspired by Spanish architecture.

LEFT
A tithe map of Kilpeck from the 1850s.

THROCKMORTON
WORCESTERSHIRE

ABOVE
An old carved corbel, possibly Saxon, inside the 13th-century church at Throckmorton.

BELOW
An avenue of trees leading to the church has been planted across part of the lost village site.

It is true that in many villages the oldest surviving structure is the church. And so it is at Throckmorton, where the chapelry dates mainly from the 13th century. However, fragments of the foundations of an earlier church have also been uncovered, although no trace remains of the wooden building that would have served the Saxon community, and which is thought to have occupied higher ground to the south west of the site.

Until 1974, Throckmorton was a chapelry of the minster at Fladbury, meaning it was subordinate to the larger church, a relationship that had probably endured from as early as AD 697. Anglo-Saxons used the word 'throc' to refer to a drain, and many believe that the name of the settlement may derive from the draining of a waterlogged marsh or moor, even though the site is situated on high ground. The area certainly contains a number of moated features, but whether these earthworks were created solely for the purposes of drainage or to denote the status of an occupier is difficult to tell.

Although omitted from the Domesday Book, probably due to its status as a chapelry, (which would have seen it listed under the entry for Fladbury), there is evidence of both

Saxon and even earlier Iron Age occupation; the latter was discovered during a three-day televised archaeological investigation that focused on the disused Pershore Airfield adjacent the present village. The excavations revealed that from Bronze Age origins a classic Iron Age settlement had developed, complete with roundhouses, enclosures and boundary ditches.

The earliest documented reference to Throckmorton comes in a charter dating to about 1020, and attributed to Wulfstan, Archbishop of Worcester and York. It refers to three 'mansae', so the village was probably already well established by this point. At that time, the bishopric of Worcester held about 80 percent of the county, including the manors of Elmley Lovett (see pages 112–113), and Bampton just to the north. By the time of Edward I (1239–1307), 35 people in the village were liable to contribute towards the Lay Subsidy Tax, paying £6 19s 8d between them, compared to Fladbury's £6 16 0d, despite the fact that the latter parish could boast twice the eligible population. In those days, arable land at Throckmorton was valued at 6d per acre, while meadow was worth four times that amount.

Proper planning
Medieval Throckmorton shows evidence of

proper planning, with a neat double row of closes running from north to south along the main village lane. Its three moated sites indicate a tripartite division of administration, perhaps relating to the three manses detailed in Wulfstan's Saxon charter. It has been suggested that later land divisions may have caused the disintegration of the community, resulting in its subsequent decay. And yet the medieval contraction of the settlement was followed by a period of expansion in the post-medieval period, with the villagers utilizing new areas of habitation. Occasionally, settlement remains from the two periods are found together, as in the earthworks to the south and east of the church, some of which can still be recognized on a 1784 Tithe map. There is evidence to suggest that the village was fully populated in 1490, but that decline may have set in shortly afterwards.

Court Farm

Throckmorton's oldest surviving secular buildings date from about 1500, and can be found at Court Farm. It belonged to the Throckmorton family, who had taken their name from the village; records show that in 1415 the Bishop of Worcester granted 14 messuages and land in Throckmorton to Sir John Throckmorton. Throckmorton Court survives largely intact, as does a timber-framed barn close by which was built at roughly the same time. Though the western service bay of the house has been lost, the medieval hall and solar (lord's chamber) remain.

Earthworks preserving the profiles of assorted ridge and furrow marks, building platforms, enclosures, hollow-ways and ponds clearly demonstrate how the village has contracted and migrated over the years. Some cottages were lost in 1940 when an airfield was constructed. While not completely deserted, Throckmorton has without doubt become a shrunken, if not entirely lost, village.

BELOW
The half-timbered Court Farm and its barn, seen here, are two of the oldest remaining buildings in the village.

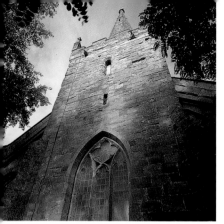

ELMLEY LOVETT
WORCESTERSHIRE

If the name of Elmley Lovett is known at all, it is likely to be as a result of the diary of Henry Townshend, a document regarded as Worcestershire's most important account of the English Civil War. The youngest son of Sir Henry Townshend, and a Royalist Commissioner for Subsidy, Henry was present at the surrender of the city of Worcester to the Parliamentary Army. He inherited the estate of Elmley Lovett from his father-in-law, Sir John Acton, the property remaining with his descendants until the 18th century.

Today, Elmley Lovett is a small hamlet in central Worcestershire, situated about 550m (600 yards) to the east of its church and medieval remains, from which it is separated by the Elmley Brook. To the north-west, a large modern trading estate crowds the earthworks of the old village, which had been abandoned by the 17th century in favour of a position closer to the main Droitwich to Kidderminster road. Soon afterwards, an avenue of trees was planted over the earthworks, an act that was likely to have been associated with Townshend's half-timbered mansion. Known as The Lodge, it was constructed in 1635 on a site 200m (220 yards) south of the church. Demolished in 1890, all that can be seen of this fine country house today is a partially walled enclosure, overgrown with vegetation, the foundations of the stables and a rubble mound thought to be the remains of a dovecote.

The earthworks of Elmley Lovett surround the churchyard of St Michael's, a church that appears to date from the 14th and 15th centuries, although the Domesday Book noted the presence of a priest on the manor in 1086. The medieval building was largely rebuilt in 1840. Beside the church lies the ringwork of the medieval manorial complex, possibly the seat of the Actons. Today it is visible only as a circular platform approximately 50m (165 feet) in diameter, and surrounded on three sides by a substantial moat that is now dry.

Elmley Lovett is an ancient settlement that appears in documents dating as far back as the 9th century. When the Domesday commissioners came calling, the community there was found to be in possession of ten plough teams, three mills and an expanse of woodland. The manor estate was in the hands of the Crown, and remained so until sold to Sir Robert Acton in 1543.

Earthwork clues

Sites of domestic buildings with their associated crofts, defined by significant banks and ditches, can be found to the south and west of the church. Further to the south is a series of irregular enclosures, within which are areas that were used for cultivation, and the remains of what might have been stock pens or huts. Access to the village from the main

road was via three hollow-ways, running east to west from the existing lane towards the church and moated site. Medieval ridge and furrow marks, can be observed to the south and east. Today, there is no trace of the medieval fishpond complex, which documentary evidence suggests comprised a chain of up to four rectangular stew ponds, visible to the south-east of the settlement until infilled by dumping in 1986. However, the large raised platform of the medieval pinfold (livestock pen) can be seen abutting the edge of the track leading to St Michael's Church and the 17th-century stone and half-timbered structure of Church Cottage.

With signs of the modern industrial and commercial landscape right on its doorstep, the village of Elmley Lovett is now protected from the pressures of redevelopment, as it has been designated a Scheduled Ancient Monument. Access to the site, which is on private land, is by two public footpaths.

BELOW
A ringwork measuring 42m (46 yards) in diameter, with a saucer-shaped top, has been mooted as a possible moated manor site.

WORMLEIGHTON
WARWICKSHIRE

ABOVE
A bishop bench-end carving found within the 12th-century church of St Peter at Wormleighton.

Not only is the depopulation of Wormleighton extremely well documented, but the results are still clearly visible on the ground today. In 1517, a government inquiry was set up to investigate acts of depopulation and enclosure that ran contrary to legislation of 1489 forbidding such practices. Consequently, John Spencer of Wormleighton was summoned to appear before the Court of Chancery. He faced the very real prospect of being forced by law to either return the many sheep pastures on his estate to arable cultivation, or forfeit half of the profits he had earned since the date of enclosure.

In the words of Richard Muir, author of *The Lost Villages of Britain*, the Spencers were one of the Tudor period's 'great sheep-based dynasties'. Towards the end of the 15th century, the family's ancestors had risen from being merely free tenants to the status of yeomen farmers, largely through the acquisition by lease or purchase of lands that either were or would soon become sheep pastures. On the backs of their many flocks the family had accrued great wealth – and not a little influence – but the consequences of John Spencer's purchase of the Wormleighton estate in 1506 threatened to stall this meteoric rise.

Spencer and the sheep

The Spencer family has often been accused of growing to prominence by evicting peasants to make way for sheep. But in the case of Wormleighton, they were innocent of that charge. For, as John Spencer argued in court, the depopulation had already occurred before he acquired Wormleighton from William Cope, a distant relative by marriage,

Cope had been cofferer of the royal household, and had purchased the lease of the Wormleighton estate from the Crown in 1498. Almost immediately, he began the task of clearing the site. Just a year after Cope acquired the estate, the occupants of 12 messuages and 3 cottages had been forcefully evicted from their homes. The land upon which the dwellings once stood, together with 97 hectares (240 acres) of arable fields, were then enclosed with hedges to create a series of pasture grounds for sheep.

BELOW
One of the largest deserted sites in Warwickshire, the site at Wormleighton comprises two rows of house-platforms, arranged on either side of a straight village street.

But it was under John Spencer's tenure that the pastures of Wormleighton came under scrutiny. The commissioners of the inquiry heard all about the 60 tearful villagers who had been turned out of their houses, the demolition of 15 homes and the subsequent decay of 12 ploughs.

Spencer had several means of defence at his disposal. Not only was he innocent of enclosing the lands, but he had subsequently built a number of new properties on the estate, including a fine new manor house. In doing so, he had provided both housing and employment for a similar number of peasants to those that had suffered at the hands of Cope.

In addition, Spencer had refurbished the church. Nevertheless, the order was given for the land to be put back under the plough. But Spencer refused to be beaten. He argued that uprooting miles of hedgerows would be very difficult – not to mention expensive. More importantly, he maintained that the hedges represented an important local resource, wood being a valuable commodity at the time. Spencer declared that it would be to the benefit of all, including the State, if the hedgerows were allowed to remain. Enclosure had increased the value of Wormleighton from £40 to £60 a year, and as a result, the rents paid to the Crown had increased from £8 to £13 per annum.

John Spencer kept his pastures, and the rise of his family continued apace; he was knighted shortly before his death in 1552. By the close of the 16th century, the Spencers had land in more than 20 parishes, all of which was largely given over to sheep. Tellingly, several of those parishes contained the sites of lost villages. It would appear, however, that Wormleighton was already a much-reduced settlement even before enclosure. At the start of the 14th century, the manor boasted 45 tenants (heads of households) and 325 hectares (800 acres) of arable land. However, by the time of Cope's evictions, the village population appears to have been cut by as much as half.

Today, the house-platforms, hollow-ways, boundaries and enclosures of Old Wormleighton are buried beneath permanent pasture below the position of the present village. Designated a 'resettled' village, Wormleighton is still considered one of the most important deserted settlement sites in Warwickshire.

ABOVE
The Gatehouse at Wormleighton. What remains of John Spencer's Hall has been converted into holiday accommodation.

BRAUNSTONBURY
AND WOLFHAMPCOTE
NORTHAMPTONSHIRE AND WARWICKSHIRE

ABOVE
*An aerial photograph of
the village sites from
January 1969.*

Two very different deserted villages in two different counties lie side by side, separated only by the River Leam. One, whose history is largely untraceable, bears all the hallmarks of a planned settlement, while the other appears to have evolved from Anglo-Saxon beginnings, its past recorded in detail since the Domesday Survey.

Braunstonbury

The earthworks of Braunstonbury village lie on level terrain at the foot of a steep hill upon which the existing village of Braunston is situated. Little can be said of its history, for the settlement was never separately taxed, while the proximity of Little Braunston and Braunston

Cleves, another deserted settlement nearby, have made the task of unravelling the manorial descent that much trickier. It is likely that Braunstonbury formed part of one of the two Braunston manors recorded in the Domesday Survey, possibly passing from the de Aincourt family to the Trusbotts before becoming part of the lands of the Abbey of Lilleshall. If this is the case, we can say with reasonable authority that at least part of Braunstonbury was still populated in 1421, when the demesne of the manor was leased.

That Braunstonbury had been deserted by the early 17th century is certain. A visitor to 'Bery-field' at that time described the village as having had 'the appearance of a ruined building', with nothing but foundations and the name Chapel Field to give any hint of its former existence.

Although battered by later activity, the Oxford Canal in the north and the construction of the London North Eastern Railway Company's embankment to the south-east, the site still clearly displays its original roughly rectangular layout. Two greens seem deliberately placed on the eastern side, and the manor house is situated neatly in the north-west corner, suggesting deliberate arrangement. The name Braunstonbury may also provide a clue, as when used in association with a manorial estate, the word 'burh' often indicates medieval town-planning.

Although some of the earthworks defy interpretation, there is a clearly defined hollow-way leading towards Braunston village, and at least five embanked closes contain small building platforms where traces of stone walls can be detected. A centrally placed two-roomed building and another large structure share a close at the centre of the site – a courtyard farm perhaps?

Village neighbour

Wolfhampcote, which at Domesday was the manor of Turchill, the Saxon Earl of Warwick, is just a short distance across the Leam. Both sides of the village's main street are lined with embanked closes, some of which display clear building platforms. Between these, narrow hollow-ways can be seen representing the alleys and side streets that once provided access to the common fields. A large octagonal moated site in the south-eastern corner is thought to be where the medieval manor house once stood, with a sizeable depression to the east identified as a possible crew yard. Further east, two parallel banks, once water-filled, may have been part of a mill complex. Strangely, there seems to be no continuation of the village's main east to west hollow-way into Braunstonbury.

Once at the heart of the village, the redundant 14th-century church of St Peter is stranded, far from the tiny hamlet that today bears the name of Wolfhampcote. Here, the 17th-century manor house, now a farm house, keeps company with an old stone tithe barn, a single cottage and the late-19th-century vicarage.

ABOVE
A ruined building at Wolfhampcote, near the church. The final depopulation of the town seems to have occurred at the turn of the 16th century.

LEFT
The view over the earthworks of Braunstonbury to the village of Braunston, which occupies a hilltop position immediately to the north east.

ABOVE
St Peter's church, Wolfhampcote. Small-scale excavation of the village site in 1955 revealed evidence for occupation between the 12th and 15th centuries.

Water and disease

Documentary evidence dating back to the end of the 11th century indicates as many as 100 people may have lived on the manor at that time, while excavations in the mid-1950s unearthed evidence of the Anglo-Saxon village of 'Ufelmescote', along with a wide array of artefacts, most of which dated from the time of peak population in the 12th and 13th centuries. Unsurprisingly, local legend maintains that the Black Death led to the village's disappearance, although evidence of sustained ditch digging for drainage and attempted road improvements

points to a community struggling against an increasingly waterlogged site in a deteriorating climate.

Much of the parish was enclosed by an Act of Parliament in the mid-18th century, but this Act post-dates the desertion of the medieval village, which probably occurred in piecemeal fashion toward the end of the 15th century, culminating in the enclosure of the common fields in 1501. Just 16 years later, the village had decayed so much that it was described as a ruin, and like its close neighbour, Braunstonbury, most of the land was given over to pasture.

THE COTTONS

NORTHAMPTONSHIRE

The Nene Way County Footpath runs for approximately 112km (70 miles) along the Northamptonshire stretch of the River Nene, from Badby to the county boundary. As it passes the town of Raunds on its way to the Kinewell Nature Reserve at Ringstead, the footpath takes walkers close to the sites of three lost villages.

There will always be sites where the documentary records let you down almost completely: Mill Cotton, Mallows Cotton, and West Cotton are three such villages. Always too small to be recorded separately from the bigger settlements nearby, the archives are largely silent on the histories of their communities. In cases such as these, it is necessary to rely even more heavily on the field archaeologist, backed up by thorough research into the general background and historical environment of the area; contrasting and comparing the available evidence with sites elsewhere in the county to give substance to hypotheses on points such as population and date of desertion.

Mallows Cotton has by far the best earthworks of the three. The village site lies on the floodplain of the River Nene at the boundary between the parishes of Raunds and Ringstead. Seven or more long, rectangular closes or crofts, bounded by banks and ditches, extend south-west towards the marshy edge of the river from a broad hollow-way that reaches a depth of 2m (6 feet) in places. At the upper end of each plot is a clearly defined building platform, with the remnants of stone walls visible here and there. To the north of the site, a lesser hollow-way follows the line of the parish boundary. Here, a large complex of substantial earthworks has been tentatively identified as a manor house and home farm.

The large circular mound in the corner, sliced in two by an excavation trench, may have been a dovecote.

Some years after his 1909 excavations on the site, C. V. Charlton wrote to the Archaeological Division of the Ordnance Survey, reporting that he had found medieval buildings at the site, rather than the Roman camp he had been expecting, and suggested that the several roundhouses uncovered 'might have been granaries'. Also among his discoveries were buildings that he interpreted as a 'stone built house with moulded door jambs', plus the charred remains of a church, on the floor of which was found a silver coin.

Mallows Cotton may have been associated with the Manor of Middle Cotes, which can be traced to the 12th century. But whatever the settlement's previous history, the Raunds enclosure map of 1798 shows that the community had definitely left by this point, as all that the document records is a group of old enclosures called 'the Cottons'.

West Cotton

About 400m (1,300 feet) to the south of Mallows Cotton, around a small tributary stream of the Nene, lies the deserted settlement of West Cotton. Evidence of Saxon habitation within dwellings of timber construction was discovered at this site, a method of building that was to give way to houses of stone by the 13th century. Excavation has also revealed signs of a medieval water mill, adding one more small piece to the puzzle of attempting to reconstruct the medieval distribution of such structures and thereby learn more about the extent of grain processing in the local area at that time.

Mill Cotton

The third of the Cottons settlements, Mill Cotton lies a short distance to the north of Mallows Cotton in the parish of Ringstead. There is evidence that a village existed here at the time of the Domesday Survey, and it may have survived into the 16th century, when it was purchased by Sir William Fitzwilliam. At some point, a moated manor house was built there. However, only fragmentary earthworks were visible when the site was surveyed in 1969, although the remnants of a mill and house abandoned earlier in the 20th century may still be seen.

By studying deserted village sites such as the Cottons, as well as those where there is more detailed evidence available, plus all contemporary villages, it is hoped that countywide settlement patterns might eventually be better understood.

SULBY
NORTHAMPTONSHIRE

I n 1831, the poet Edward Fitzgerald (1809–83) briefly lodged at a farmhouse on the site of the Battle of Naseby, which was fought in 1645 at the height of the English Civil War. The site clearly captured his not inconsiderable imagination, as he returned in 1842, this time searching for the centre of the battlefield and, while digging into a curious-looking mound, he unearthed numerous skeletons. This mass grave was on the western edge of the battlefield, and it seemed that he had found the Civil War cemetery of legend. However, he was no longer in the parish of Naseby, but had crossed the invisible border into Sulby.

Sulby is a small, flat, triangular parish of just 650 hectares (1,600 acres). It has Leicestershire on its north-west boundary, and the beginnings of the River Avon to the south-west. As well as the possible war grave, the area can claim two other historic landmarks.

Two Sulbys

At the time of the Domesday Survey there were two manors in Sulby parish. The first was owned by Geoffrey de Wirce. It was small – just two and a half hides – and was described as 'waste'. Could this have been the site of an abandoned Saxon settlement? We may never know, for it was soon home to the Premonstraterian canons of the Sulby Abbey. Originally founded in neighbouring Welford, nine carucates (parcels of land) from Sulby were included in its original endowment. A short time afterwards, however, the abbey received an additional grant of a manor in Sulby – perhaps de Wirce's 'waste' – and also the parish church. This prompted a move, and the abbey occupied a site on the south-east edge of Sulby parish until it was dissolved in 1538. Although never large – the number of canons never exceeded 13 in the 15th century – Edward II (1284–1387) stayed at the abbey several times.

In 1086, it was documented that the second Sulby manor was in the possession of one Guy de Reinbuedcurt. With a recorded population of 13, it lay on sloping ground at the western edge of the parish, north-west of a tributary of the River Avon. From about 1215, the manor was in the hands of Sulby Abbey. The village contributed a reasonable amount – 31 shillings – to the Lay Subsidy of 1334, and by 1377, 89 people, or approximately 30 households, were liable for the Poll Tax. However, by 1428 a mere four households were counted, and in 1451 it was reported that the nave of the parish church of St Botolph had collapsed. It seems that the rest of the church came down during the dissolution of the monasteries in the 1530s, at which time it was recorded that the canons of Sulby Abbey were grazing 2,000 sheep in a close called Old Soulby. Evasion aside, it appears there were just five householders in Sulby village when the Hearth Tax was collected in 1674. By the early 18th century, it was reported that there were only a few scattered houses left.

Discovering the village

The deserted medieval village of Old Sulby remained well and truly lost for

BELOW
A 17th-century bridge crosses the stream that runs through the grounds of Park Farm and along the eastern edge of the site to Sulby Reservoir.

some time. With no church to guide the investigators, they searched at Sulby Hall, Sulby Lodge, Sulby Covert and Sulby Grange, all without success. It was not until a Dr St. Joseph, then Lecturer in Geology at Cambridge University, took some aerial photographs of the parish that the ploughed-over but still well-preserved earthworks were located west of Park Farm.

Sulby's broad main hollow-way, which is 1m (3 feet) deep in places, runs from north to south at the west of the site. Building platforms within embanked enclosures can be seen on either side, and behind them long enclosures acted as allotments for the householders. There is a second hollow-way running at right angles to the first, crossing the centre of the surviving earthworks with a similar but more irregular series of tofts and crofts beside it. At the junction of the two

'streets' is a large enclosure, measuring 40m (130 feet) by 30m (100 feet). Roughly rectangular in shape, and defined by ditches 2m (6 feet) deep, it could be the site of St Botolph's Church, as the platform is oriented east to west and rises approximately 1.5m (5 feet) above the surrounding ground level.

The remains of the late medieval ridge and furrow that overlies most of the site suggests that Sulby was completely ploughed over after it was deserted, and that fields and village alike were used for arable cultivation. By the 16th century, Sulby had become a pasture. Just a single short petition to the chancellor seems to mark the demise of Sulby village; the Abbot of Sulby complained that he was suffering a loss of rents because, 'the fields were used with tillage and nowe the said towns be pulled down and laid to pasture…'

COLD NEWTON

LEICESTERSHIRE

Cold Newton is a perfect example of how misleading population statistics can be when trying to identify abandoned village sites. While not strictly deserted, the village has undoubtedly been severely reduced, not to mention widely redistributed. But, as the historian W. G. Hoskins noted, the extent of the area abandoned at Cold Newton is comparable to that of many fully depopulated settlements. With possible sites for a medieval manor house, moat, fishpond, trackways, a windmill and even a chapel, it certainly has much to offer the seeker of lost villages.

Aptly named

Until the 1420s, the village was officially known as Newton Burdit. But cold is something Newton certainly was, situated on a ridge of the Liassic clay uplands 152m (500 feet) above sea level and exposed to the wind from all sides. No doubt after many years of local usage the popular name eventually stuck.

As a chapelry, probably the daughter settlement of nearby Lowesby, Cold Newton's implied Danish ancestry places its origins no earlier than the end of the 10th century. With 11 households at the time the Domesday Book was compiled, it appears always to have been a settlement on a modest scale. Yet, despite its small size, Cold Newton displays remarkable stability, with an estimated 11 households in 1337 and 12 to 15 households – about 60 inhabitants – in 1377. The figures don't seem to vary much after that. A diocesan return of 1563 and the hearth tax assessment of 1670 both imply a community of around 15 households. Even more perplexing is the figure for the first census in 1801, when the so-called 'shrunken' village of Cold Newton returned a figure of 101 inhabitants for the chapelry.

On paper, it is difficult to see where any abandonment, desertion or shrinkage has taken place, but stand on top of that blustery ridge 13 km (8 miles) from Leicester and the evidence stretches out before you.

Eyewitness evidence

Enclosure took place some time before the end of the 16th century and was largely complete before 1641. The process was gradual and saw the redistribution of villagers from a central village core surrounded by open fields to a dispersed scatter of individual farmsteads among the newly defined pasture lands. This movement created an abandoned village site with no actual fall in figures for the population of the manor as a whole.

The manor house itself seems to have migrated from its dry-moated homestead site to its present position at the elbow of the gated Skeg Hill Road, which leads to Lowesby (the site of another deserted village). Now a farmhouse, the structure exhibits several 16th-century features and is actually called Manor House Farm. At one time pieces of worked stone and large Swithland roofing-slates could be seen strewn near the northern edge

of the moated platform on which the original manor or grange complex stood, but much of this has now been cleared away.

North of the present village it is possible to trace almost the whole of Cold Newton's street pattern on the ground. The main street, a continuation of the modern road, now takes the form of a prominent north to south hollow-way with many subsidiary trackways branching off and running between identifiable crofts and house platforms. The chapel site has been less easy to pin down, but it is likely to have been within the pasture known as Chapel Hill Field. A further set of earthworks to the east of Skeg Hill Road contains mostly minor trackways and a series of irregular house platforms. It also includes a well-defined square moat. Just 170 m (550 feet) north of this site is a circular windmill mound. Another area south of the present village also displays hollow-ways and house platforms.

Cold Newton is as intriguing as it is extensive. The site is a Scheduled Ancient Monument, with access via several footpaths across private farmland.

BELOW

Although no structures from the medieval village survive, weathered stone, presumably from the ruins of the chapel, was used to create a drinking-place for cattle in Chapel Hill Field.

INGARSBY

LEICESTERSHIRE

I ngarsby is rare among deserted villages, for the exact year of its final depopulation is known. The settlement was probably founded by a Danish individual named Ingwar, and as such was referred to as 'Ingwar's village', or Ingarsby. This places its origins, in all likelihood, at some point in the 10th century, although dating a site by its name is problematic.

Final years

The Domesday Book reports 32 heads of households present in Ingarsby in 1086, suggesting that there may have been around 150 inhabitants altogether. This is certainly more than could be claimed by a number of other lost villages. Yet this relative prosperity was not to last, for by 1334, the manor had one of the lowest tax quotas in the county at just 9 shillings. Three years later, a mere decade before the arrival of the Black Death, there appear to have been no more than a dozen families in residence. We have no way of knowing how the tiny Ingarsby community suffered during the plague years, but The Pestilence, however terrible, did not prove to be the final depopulating force for this village, although it may well have precipitated the end. That arrived five years later, when Simon Islip, Archbishop of Canterbury, granted Leicester Abbey all but 12 holdings at Ingarsby. Whatever the villagers made of the news at the time, the event spelled doom for their community.

Between 1377–81, it was recorded that there were 32 taxpayers in the village, plus an unknown quantity of non-taxpayers, which was roughly the same number of inhabitants that had lived there 40 years earlier. But how many of these people still lived in the village itself and toiled in its fields? Alternatively, how many might now be found at the new complex of estate buildings?

One by one, Leicester Abbey bought out the surviving freeholders, and by 1469 it owned the entire manorial estate. Next, the costly process of enclosing all the lands of Ingarsby with hedges and ditches began. Meanwhile, as the open fields were converted into pasture for sheep and cattle, the old moated manor house was redeveloped as a grange farm, and became the residence of one of the canons of the abbey who took the title of Prior of the Grange.

Of course there may have been no other course of action left open to the abbey. With

only a small and possibly diminishing work-force, the vast open fields would quickly have become unmanageable. But with the exception of those occupying the new grange buildings, the enclosure of 1469 resulted in complete depopulation of the village. Some arable land was retained, and a mill that had been operational at Ingarsby since 1086 continued to function in one form or another until 1599, many years after the village had disappeared. Part of the estate was also leased for grazing to a family named Ashby from nearby Lowesby.

By the time of the Dissolution of the Monasteries in the 16th century, Leicester Abbey was deeply in debt. Nevertheless, it was one of the few such religious institutions to survive – it managed to hold onto the chapel at Ingarsby, but lost the grange, which was considered the most valuable property of its kind in Leicestershire at that time. It was eventually sold for £1,371 6s 8d to one Brian Cave. His family soon took up residence in their new home at Ingarsby, but, apart from their servants and labourers,

they were the only inhabitants – the village had long gone.

Although visible on both sides of Ingarsby Lane (the Houghton to Hungerton road), the main area of earthworks occupies a west-facing slope that dips down to a small, clear stream. A hollow-way, which would once have served as the main street of the old village, follows a footpath that leads to the nearby hamlet of Billesdon Coplow and the village of Tilton on the Hill. Numerous side streets branch off along its length, between which can be seen rectangular house-platforms, with their spacious garden closes or orchard grounds. The southern village boundary can still be traced as a substantial bank and ditch that is more than 3m (10 feet) deep and 10m (30 feet) wide, while other features, such as hollow-ways, fish ponds, stock enclosures and even a mill pond, have been identified at various points around the site. For a medieval village deserted as long ago as 1469, the earthworks of Ingarsby remain remarkably distinct and striking.

HEATH
SHROPSHIRE

Hidden away among a maze of narrow, sunken lanes on the lower slopes of Brown Clee Hill lie the deserted medieval villages of Cold Weston, Abdon, Norncott and Heath. Roads between the sites pass through sparsely populated farmland spotted with sheep, and with virtually no passing cars, the sense of isolation is only broken when occasional gaps between the tall trees reveal the spectacular views over Corve Dale.

Extending over an area of more than 4 hectares (10 acres), immediately to the north of a tiny Norman chapel, the earthworks of the lost village of Heath are perhaps the most visible and easily accessible of this group of abandoned settlement sites. Yet extensive as the earthworks are here, there were just seven families at Heath who were liable to pay tax in 1327, while a plan drawn in the early 1770s shows just four tenements on the estate. This same document helpfully reveals the layout of the former village, recording the pattern of roads and tracks around which the houses, outbuildings, gardens, enclosures and ponds were arranged. Also marked on the plan was a multi-sided, ditched enclosure to the north-west of the chapel, which is thought to represent a manorial complex, although it is referred to on the plan simply as 'Moat Meadow'. Up until that point at least, it would see, there were still some buildings standing at Heath.

A lonely chapel

The chapel that once served the community of Heath village now stands alone in a roadside field. Consisting of just a nave and chancel, the building has altered little since it was built

BELOW
The earthworks of the lost medieval village lie in a field to the north-west of the chapel.

ABOVE
A typically Norman round-arched door on an almost unspoiled example of rural architecture dating from nearly nine centuries ago.

internal bank and a few building platforms within clearly defined 'courts' can now be made out. Construction of a late-18th-century farm house, which is also no longer standing, disturbed the earthworks of the eastern arm of the moat, and two further post-medieval farm houses, one of which survives as Heath House, have also encroached on the wider manorial area. To the west lies a substantial fishpond, which may once have formed the pond bay of a watermill, and a small, circular, stone-lined well can be found nearby.

Between the main body of the settlement and a hollow-way that is followed by the northern boundary of the field, faint traces of earthworks indicate where modern ploughing has destroyed other remains. However, areas of ridge and furrow, which once made up part of the great open field known long ago as 'Wynet', are still easy to detect in the outlying areas to the east, south and west. Heath also possessed a deer park, its extent defined today only by modern field boundaries.

Fatal consequences

In 1954, only one probable deserted village site was known in the county, but following the work of the Shropshire Deserted Medieval Settlement Project in the late 1980s, more than 100 sites of abandoned habitation areas have been identified, several of them, as already noted, situated in the vicinity of Heath. The usual depopulating pressures of the late Middle Ages probably apply to most of these sites. The effects of plague, shifting economic circumstances and migration from settlements that were already quite small were all exaserbated by the clamour for wool. Each of these causes could have been survived individually, but when combined, the consequences were catastrophic for many communities.

almost 900 years ago. Unable to extend or enhance the structure over the years, as a wealthier community may have been tempted to do, the inhabitants of Heath have left us with a near-perfect example of simple, rural 12th-century ecclesiastical design.

The former appearance of the Moat Meadow complex can only be guessed at, however, as only the central moat itself, an

STOKESAY
SHROPSHIRE

Stokesay Castle, on the banks of the River Onny, is one of Shropshire's most popular tourist attractions. Thousands flock here each year to admire the carvings above the entrance to its gatehouse and the wonderful oak beams of the great hall. However, few visitors to the place realize that a medieval village once stood in its shadow.

Called Stoches at the time of the Domesday Survey, a name that originally denoted an 'outlying farmstead or hamlet'; the village later acquired the suffix 'say' from the de Saye family who had arrived in England with William the Conqueror, and were the tenant lords of Stokesay from 1105 until 1240.

Stokesay has been altered and added to over the centuries, but it retains a remarkable number of original features. The oldest part of the building is the Norman north tower, which may have been built as a Marcher pelé-tower, or defensive residence, for the de Saye family in the years before the border lands between England and Wales were finally subdued. In 1150, the de Sayes added a chapel to their stronghold, much of which can still be seen in the fabric of Stokesay church.

When the leading Shrewsbury merchant Lawrence Ludlow took over the manor in 1281, he constructed a magnificent timber-framed great hall, kitchen block and solar (private chamber), and surrounded the castle with a water-filled moat. He subsequently walled the courtyard, and was granted a licence to crenellate the building in 1291. Although the threat from the Welsh had decreased significantly by this point, it is surely no accident that Stokesay looks at its most imposing and formidable when viewed from the west. However, the fortifications were largely a symbol of status rather than a measure for defence. It has been suggested that in the Middle Ages, the principal road through the village may have passed on the building's western side.

Medieval Shropshire was at the centre of the booming wool trade, contributing more than half of England's wool exports in 1273. This was the means by which Ludlow accrued his vast fortune, his wealth buying status far above his actual position as feudal tenant. In 1281 he even managed to obtain a coveted royal charter of free hunting rights.

Pasture and depopulation

However, while Ludlow's place in the history of the county is well known, we have almost no information regarding the fate of the Domesday community of Stoches.

ABOVE
This beautiful carving on the timber-framed gate-house was built in the 17th century to replace an earlier example.

BELOW
Stokesay Castle is a rare example of the classic medieval fortified residence.

RIGHT

Seen here from the adjacent churchyard, Stokesay Castle is a fortified manor house built in the 13th century. The Great Hall survives virtually intact, although the wet moat that once surrounded it is now dry.

The same Roger holds STOKESAY. Ealdraed held it and was a free man. There are 7 hides paying gold. There is land for 14 ploughs. In demesne were 5 ploughs and 16 slaves and female slaves together; and 20 villans with 8 ploughs, and 9 female cottars. There is a mill rendering 9 summae of wheat, and there is a miller and a bee-keeper. TRE it was worth £10.

THE DOMESDAY BOOK

From the early 14th century, there is evidence of piecemeal and trouble-free enclosure throughout the county; by the 16th century, Shropshire was largely enclosed.

Perhaps Stokesay was always much as it is today, a church and manor house grouping, with a loosely associated collection of farms and smallholdings. Areas of early enclosure are often believed to have been immune from the forces of later medieval depopulation, largely because their communities were already well dispersed and settled. Whether the original Stokesay dwindled to nothing as the pasture grew in size under Shropshire's greatest wool man, or whether the settlement merely migrated to its present position is unknown. An entry in the accounts of the manor bailiff in 1424–25 records the proceeds of 'the sale of herbage of several closes and of frisc [uncultivated] land in one of the common fields', indicating that areas of pasture had infiltrated the arable land, albeit temporarily, and that some peasants still lived in the area, shown by the presence of common land.

Lawrence Ludlow only lived to enjoy his grand manor house for a few short years, but his family retained the property for three more centuries, their eventual successors being the Cravens.

Incredibly, Stokesay survived the English Civil War virtually intact. Although the outer wall and much of the church were destroyed, it is said that the occupants of the house so loved it that they preferred to surrender it to the enemy rather than see it damaged. However, by the beginning of the 19th century decay had set in, and a nearby farm was using parts of the property. But Stokesay was not without friends. Efforts to effect some kind of restoration began in the 1850s, and by the end of the following decade the house had been bought by J. D. Alcroft, who initiated sympathetic repairs and refurbishment. Under the auspices of the Alcrofts, the castle was opened to the public in 1908. Since 1992, the property has been in the care of English Heritage. This unique old manor house should be safe for many years more, but old Stokesay village has been lost without a trace.

WYCHNOR
STAFFORDSHIRE

ABOVE
In the church of St Leonard, 17th century stained glass sits within a much older frame.

ABOVE
In the church of St Leonard, 17th century stained glass sits within a much older frame.

I n 1973, an archaeologist named S. Losco-Bradley began excavations at Catholme, near the confluence of the rivers Trent, Tame and Mease, and unearthed part of a large middle-Saxon settlement. Traces of 65 separate buildings were uncovered amid a system of ditched tracks and enclosures. Heading north-east, along a continuation of the same gravel terrace on the north bank of the River Trent, quarrying at Wychnor revealed a pagan-Anglo-Saxon cemetery, along with evidence for a Romano-British community.

Today, there is little in the way of a settlement at either of these two locations. In fact, things were not much different in 1086, for when the Domesday commissioners visited Wychnor they found just four villagers, two smallholders, a mill and a church. By 1164, the moated Wychnor Hall was in the hands of the Somervilles, and by the later Middle Ages, the settlement seems to have expanded.

March 1322 saw the village caught up in an act of insurrection. Thomas, the 2nd Earl of Lancaster (1278–1322), organized a rebellion against Edward II (1284–1327). To try to prevent the king from crossing the River Trent two men, John de Myner, Master Forester of Needwood Forest, and Richard de Holland, broke down bridges at Wychnor and Ridware. However, Edward found an alternative route and was in time to crush Lancaster's forces at the Battle of Burton Bridge. Richard de Holland was subsequently fined a hefty 40 shillings for the damage to the bridges.

John of Gaunt's bacon

In the early 1330s, Sir Philip Somerville held the manor of Wychnor from John of Gaunt,

BELOW
An aerial view of Wychnor, from May 1965. The building of the canal destroyed part of the site of the moated Wychnor Hall.

(1340–99), a man who seemed to delight in thinking up bizarre customs for his tenants to perform at their manors. At Wychnor, Gaunt called for the Lord of the Manor to keep a flitch (side) of bacon hanging in his hall all year round, except during Lent. Local villagers could then compete for this prize in a particularly novel way. To qualify, the claimants must have been married for a year and a day without ever having quarrelled or regretted the union. They also had to swear that if they were single, they would still choose the same partner. In order to prove their eligibility, two witnesses had to be found who could vouch for the veracity of the couple's story. Should anyone win the bacon, which came with a few extras, such as a cheese and a quarter of wheat, the prize would be paraded before them, carried in front of a procession of minstrels and trumpeters, prior to being transported to the winner's house. It was said that only three couples ever met the stipulated criteria. One couple apparently argued over how best to cook the meat and were promptly asked to give it back; another pair had not seen each other since the day of their marriage, as the husband was a sailor; the third couple consisted of a good-natured man whose wife was unable to speak! When years passed with no successful applicants, the flitch of bacon was replaced with a wooden replica, which was hung in the village as a cautionary reminder of the realities of marriage.

While the truth of this tale may be in some doubt, the reality of medieval Wychnor is written in its earthworks. The site is now a Scheduled Ancient Monument, and has been divided into four areas. In the centre and towards the east, the hollowways are bounded by raised platforms, while to the north there are further raised platforms, along with various banks and ditches. In the west are field boundaries and ridge and furrow patterns, while to the south is the site of the Somervilles' moated manor house, which was demolished in 1535. The old hall is believed to have begun to decay because its riverside position made it liable to flooding. Nearby there is another moated enclosure and a series of medieval fishponds. Construction started on a new manor house in 1584, apparently in a less watery location. Sadly, the site of the original house was damaged in the 1770s, when the Trent and Mersey canal was cut through the village, heralding the new industrial era.

TATTON
CHESHIRE

At the turn of the 17th century, Sir Thomas Egerton (1540–1617), who was then Chancellor of England, inherited Tatton. He began a family connection with the estate that lasted for more than 350 years. In 1959, a bequest in the will of Maurice Egerton left Tatton Park to the National Trust, which assumed care of a fine Georgian mansion set amid some 400 hectares (1,000 acres) of landscaped parkland. Of the old medieval village of Tatton Green, however, there was barely a trace.

People had been living at Tatton and cultivating the well-drained soils of the Rostherne Ridge since at least 350 BC. Excavations have uncovered the foundation trenches and post holes of a Romano-British farm, the site of which may have been inhabited right up until early Saxon times. But as a frontier settlement troubled by raids and tribal skirmishes, the village then seems to have experienced something of a hiatus. It was during the peaceful years leading up to the Norman Conquest that Tatton really established itself as a significant village community, with its houses gathered around a farmstead complex.

By 1066 the lands belonging to Tatton represented the largest agricultural area of any settlement on the Rostherne Ridge, its four ploughlands divided unequally between two manors. The smaller lordship, which was extensively wooded, eventually developed into a secondary settlement known as Norshaw, with enough land for just half a plough. Miraculously, the two Tatton manors appear to have escaped the Norman wasting of northeast Cheshire, and by the time of the Domesday Book a combined population of between 70–100 people inhabited the settlements. Tatton Green, the larger of the two villages, developed from its Saxon precursor into a loose assemblage of agricultural and domestic timber structures. Together with the associated parcels of land, its site sits close beside a trackway that formed part of the original road from Rostherne to Knutsford.

During the course of the 12th century, as the pattern of landholding grew more and more fragmented, so the physical aspect of the village became increasingly compartmentalized by the construction of numerous banks and ditches. It was at about this time that Mobberley Priory acquired land at Tatton, around which they erected protective fences. This became an estate called Hazelhurst, and was later purchased by Robert de Massey, who turned it into a park. As a result, the Knutsford Road was diverted around the enclosed land.

Studies of the surviving earthworks from the medieval village indicate that it consisted of a village green and approximately 15 houses, which were strung out along the southern 'Portstrete' (Market Street) section of the main thoroughfare, the market in question being that at Knutsford. The old Saxon farmstead had been replaced by a new farm complex that fronted the main lane and contained a yard, barns and stock enclosures, as well as a house, which lay end-on to the street. Off to

the west, east and north of the settlement stretched the common grazing land and the ridge and furrow of the open fields. Although farming at Tatton was mixed – a combination of arable, sheep and pigs – the importance of flocks and their fleeces to the village economy is evident in field names such as 'Chepfaldde furluc' and 'Sepefurllong furlong', as well as in the plentiful evidence of fulling (cloth processing) activities. Even so, failing grain markets in the 14th century seem to have encouraged the engrossment and consolidation of the numerous individual holdings on the Tatton estate. Pottery evidence indicates that the roadside part of the village was abandoned towards the end of the 14th century, reflecting both a nationwide contraction in population and a local reorganization of resources.

Old Hall

It has also been suggested that the construction of a large house to the south of the village may have accelerated the desertion of the roadside buildings. But Old Hall, as it was later known, was probably built around 1460, some time after desertion is believed to have taken place. No trace has yet been found of the earlier 'hallmote', if it ever existed. Originally a U- or E- shaped construction, the Old Hall stood with its open side facing the village green. In the late-16th century, a limited amount of resettling seems to have taken place in the area immediately to the north of the big house, but these new crofts appear to have completely shunned the sites of the previous structures. At the same time, a rationalization of the open fields was underway.

An increase in population during the Tudor period put renewed pressure on land and resources, at a level unknown since the decades before the Black Death. Twenty-six people were listed in the Lay Subsidy Roll for 1542, a figure that rose to about 35 by the 1670s. Some of the farm leases at Tatton came with entry fines to the tune of £100–£150, suggesting that the main tenants of the larger farms were relatively affluent. But the parish registers seem to indicate that

many of the peasants did not hold enough land to sustain their families, as occupations such as carpenter, fuller, tailor, innkeeper, blacksmith, farrier, sawyer and slater occur with ever increasing frequency.

Upon inheriting the estate, Sir Thomas Egerton did not live at Tatton. Instead, he leased it to his nephew, John Egerton, who, unimpressed with the Old Hall, set about constructing a fine new residence on part of the demesne of the manor.

ABOVE
Now overgrown with thistles and grasses, 'Portstrete' was once the road to market. Having crossed a stream, it led through fields, pastures and woodland to the village of Knutsford.

ABOVE

A view of the now sunken 'Portstrete', with Tatton Old Hall in the distance on the right.

Tatton Park

The 1730s saw the beginning of a 20-year agricultural depression that hit the estate hard, and for a while it appeared as though Tatton, or at least part of it, would have to be sold. A map of Tatton Park drawn in 1733, when much of the estate was leased to a family named Harrison, shows a village in decline, with just a dozen or so scattered houses, barns and other buildings in addition to the Old Hall complex, its open fields almost totally enclosed with banks and hedges. But just 24 years later, there were reports that these hedges were being torn up, as the Egertons took more and more land in hand, bought up leases and went about the business of turning the estate into a vast park. By 1784, William Egerton was the sole landowner at Tatton, and less than a decade later, with the financial assistance of a wealthy uncle, Sam Hill of Shenstone, in Staffordshire, Tatton was transformed into a magnificent park.

Just why the Egertons embarked on such an ambitious plan at a time when their financial position at Tatton was so insecure is a subject that warrents closer inspection. As with most depopulations and major shifts in land use, a number of factors were at work. Rent arrears on the Egerton lands were running at £650 in 1745, and it appears that many of the tenants were struggling. As the agricultural depression continued, the north-west was dealt a second blow, with outbreaks of cattle plague. Excavated live-stock burials at the old village site dating to the mid-18th century suggest that this may have been a problem at Tatton. With income from the estate falling, yet no reduction in maintenance costs, turning the estate into parkland was perhaps an appealing option. In addition, Samuel Egerton, who held the property in 1739, was named guardian to the young Francis Egerton, 3rd Duke of Bridgwater, and placed in temporary administrative control of the vast Bridgwater estate. This task allowed him to mix within higher society, exposing him to a way of life from which the financial state of Tatton had excluded him.

Thousands of visitors now marvel at the magnificent Georgian mansion, wandering across the rolling parkland and through the award-winning gardens. It is only when they reach the Tudor Old Hall, and perhaps notice the perplexing grooves and banks under the grass, that they might wonder what could have been there before.

ALKMONTON AND HUNGRY BENTLEY

DERBYSHIRE

The high number of deserted and shrunken villages in the Derbyshire Dales indicates that the medieval density of settlement in the region was considerably greater than it is today. For example, situated just to the north of a Roman road once called Long Lane are the remains of the former liberty of Hungry Bentley. The remnants of this deserted settlement include a group of well-preserved earthworks and an associated field system. Only 3.2km (2 miles) distant, a large field immediately to the north of Alkmonton Old Hall Farm protects the remnants of the medieval streets, houses and chapel of the abandoned part of Alkmonton village.

A medieval hospital

Recorded as 'Alchementune' in the Domesday Book, the manor of Alkmonton was owned by one Henry de Ferieres. Along with its taxable value of 40 shillings, it was noted that there was land for two ploughs, as well as 4.85 hectares (12 acres) of meadow and woodland for pannage. Not long after, in 1100, Robert de Bakepuze of Barton Bakepuze, later renamed Barton Blount (see pages 140–141), founded a hospital for female lepers between Alkmonton and Bentley, which he dedicated to St Leonard.

During the reign of Richard II (1367–1400), the Blount family took up residence at Barton, having purchased the ancient estates of the Bakepuze family when the last member of its male line died. This acquisition included the manor of Alkmontune which, if the sizeable amount of tax it paid in 1334 is anything to go by, was easily as large as any of its neighbours. Sir Walter Blount was the king's standard bearer, and three years after his death at the battle of Shrewsbury, in 1403, his widow re-founded the hospital at Alkmonton, although leprosy was on the wane by this time. This additional endowment was sufficient to maintain a chaplain, who was employed to pray for her soul and for those of her family.

St Leonard's was further endowed by the will of Sir Walter's great-grandson, the first Lord Mountjoy, who bequeathed land and changed the nature of the ancient hospital. Thenceforth, it was to operate as a charity for

ABOVE
St John's church, at Alkmonton, is some distance from the site of the original village.

BELOW
An ancient Ash tree is growing in through the old sunken road at Alkmonton.

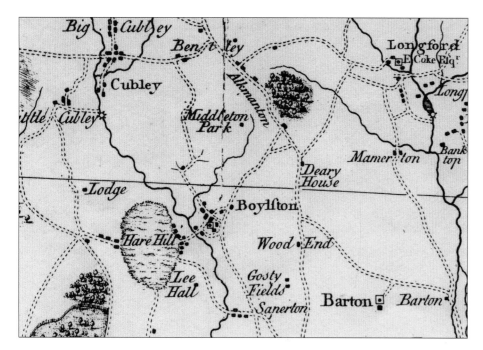

ABOVE
Burdett's 1791 Map of Derbyshire, showing the relative positions of the much shrunken settlements of 'Bentley' and 'Alkmanton'.

seven poor men over the age of 55, who were old retainers from the family's estates. There was also provision for the building of a chapel dedicated to St Nicholas, where the master of the hospital was to say an annual mass. However, in the reign of Edward VI (1537–53), the 'spittle house' of Alkmonton, together with its 'many adjacent closes and meadows', was sold to John Bellowe and Edward Streetbury for £121 3s 8d. There is no indication as to what became of the seven poor pensioners, although the hospital was not finally abolished until after the Reformation.

Surrounded by open fields, the main focus of this settlement seems to have been a small village green that could be approached via four separate sunken tracks. Forming a kind of back lane, the north-east track simply led out to the ridge and furrow fields. It is still clearly visible today, as are four identifiable medieval furlongs, complete with traces of individual strips and headlands. A large terraced platform nearby is thought to have been the site of St Nicholas's Chapel; a Norman font, now kept in the parish church, was excavated at the site in the 1960s, while crop marks have revealed the location of a long, narrow building. The three remaining tracks were each lined with banked and ditched enclosures that even now con-

tain traces of building platforms. On the edge of the occupied area, a steep, narrow gully was discovered. It leads to a small depression in a field to the south of the site, and was formed by a stream running into a pond, which is now completely dry.

About a kilometre to the north, some resettlement has occurred. This later Alkmonton village grew up around St John's Church, which was restored in 1878 by the Evans family, who were the lords of the manor and sole landowners of the settlement at that time. Oddly, the church is actually closer to the deserted medieval village of Hungry Bentley than it is to its own departed predecessor.

Hungry Bentley
Bentley, thought to derive from the Old English words 'beonet', meaning bent grass, and 'leah', meaning clearing, is a common-place name in this area. Therefore, to distinguish it from the other Bentleys, a descriptive prefix was added – the choice of 'Hungry' indicating that the soil here was reputed to be of poor quality.

While medieval Alkmonton occupied the gently undulating ground of a south-west facing slope, Hungry Bentley, to the east of Bentley Brook, was situated on a much steeper incline of identical orientation, which afforded commanding views of the valley. In 1086, the Domesday Commissioners found land for just one plough at 'Beneleie', as it was then known, and the taxable worth of the manor, at that time in the same hands as its larger neighbour, Alkmonton, was assessed at 11 shillings.

Hungry Bentley is renowned as the most impressive depopulated settlement site in Derbyshire. It was formed along a central sunken track that runs east to west, more or less parallel to the nearby Roman road. Clearly visible on both sides is an irregular series of roughly rectangular enclosures that are bounded by distinct banks and ditches. Around half a dozen of these tofts contain features that are likely to have been building platforms, and may once have borne dwellings. A second series of enclosures towards the western end of the track show traces of ridge and furrow formations. Even further west, two enclosures have been partly terraced into the sloping ground; one contains ridge and furrow marks, while the other could have been a stock enclosure. To the south, situated between the village earthworks and Long Lane, is the site of a medieval homestead moat. This surrounds the surviving traces of Bentley Hall, an Elizabethan or Jacobean house which, along with the settlement remains, has been designated a Scheduled Ancient Monument.

By the late 16th century, Bentley Hall was occupied by the Bentley Family. In 1586, Edward Bentley of Hungry Bentley was tried and convicted of high treason at the Old Bailey.

As at Alkmonton, the reasons for the village's eventual depopulation remain obscure. Pestilence has been mooted, but, as is the case with other sites, this was rarely the sole cause of a desertion, and it is likely that a move from arable to pastoral farming, as well as a deteriorating climate, also played their part. The sites of both these villages are today on private farmland, but while Hungry Bentley can be reached by public footpath, there is no access to Alkmonton, and nothing can be seen from the very sunken Leaply Lane that runs alongside.

BELOW
View looking west from site of the lost village of Alkmonton.

BARTON BLOUNT

DERBYSHIRE

ABOVE
Barton [Blount] as depicted on Burdett's 1791 Map of Derbyshire.

BELOW
Within the landscaped grounds of Barton Hall, the old village church of St Chad was rebuilt in 1714 using medieval masonry.

W hen Walter Blount, the first Lord Mountjoy, died in 1474, he was in possession of no less than 42 manors in six different counties. One of them was Barton Blount, which was situated on the undulating clay of South Derbyshire, and where the medieval village was possibly in the last stages of decay. Formerly named Barton Bakepuze, after the family that had owned the estate from the 13th century, its name changed when it was purchased by Lord Mountjoy's great-grandfather, Sir Walter Blount, in 1381.

When the Domesday Survey was being compiled in 1086, the manor was called 'Barctune', and had already been occupied for at least a century, as indicated by fragments of Saxon pottery recovered from the site. It was owned by Henry de Ferieres, and was already of considerable size. Worth a total of £4, the estate comprised extensive plough lands, 25 hectares (64 acres) of meadow, plus a church and two mills. Excavations in the late 1960s and early 1970s revealed that Barton Blount had undergone at least five phases of expansion before its eventual depopulation at some time in the 15th century.

Early peasant-houses of the 'clay land' villages such as Barton Blount were constructed from timber and unbaked earths or cob. Preliminary excavations at the site in 1968 uncovered a sequence of different timber buildings which dated from the 12th to the 14th centuries, and displayed changes in construction methods. They also revealed the first recorded example in the Midlands of a shift in alignment through 90°. The reasons behind such shifts in orientation remain unclear, but evidence from around the country proves that they were neither regional nor chronological, and seem to have been local responses to specific circumstances.

Several groups of crofts and tofts have been discovered at Barton Blount, about half a dozen of which are situated on either side of the pronounced sunken track that formed the main street of the village. Most of these enclosures are defined by low banks and ditches, but just north of the track, the largest platform has steep banks surviving to a height of up to 1m (3 feet) in places. A sunken track runs north-east from the northern corner, while another runs from the main street and forms a back lane to the open fields, abutting the crofts to the south-east. Still in use today, the track is defined by a double field boundary.

All around the site, the elongated reverse 's' lines of the ridge and furrow cultivation strips remain clear to see.

Six of the medieval houses at Barton Blount had crew yards, in which cattle would have been overwintered. This appears to have been a late development in the village, emerging in the mid- to late-14th century. It is possible that a change from arable to pastoral farming contributed to the decline of the settlement, because animal husbandry required fewer hands. The next century saw the construction of an impressive semi-fortified moated manor house, Barton Hall, alongside the medieval church of St Chad's, once at the heart of the settlement. It also saw the final depopulation of the village.

In the middle of the 16th century, James, the 6th Lord Mountjoy, sold some of the Blount estates, including Barton Blount. During the English Civil War of the 1640s, a Parliamentary garrison was positioned there in opposition to the Royalist garrison at nearby Tutbury. It was then that St Chad's was badly damaged. So dilapidated had it become by 1714 that it was rebuilt, re-using much of the medieval masonry. A second rebuilding occurred 1845, but a 14th-century effigy and the late medieval font remain.

Duck decoy

Barton Hall has been altered over the years, with part of its moat filled in when the grounds were landscaped. Luckily, the medieval decoy pond survived. Dug from the natural clay about 150m (490 feet) south-west of the Hall, it measures some 100m (320 feet) by 60m (200 feet), with a central island of about 25m (80 feet) in diameter. Ducks and other waterfowl were lured with bait, or driven up a tapering narrow channel called a 'pipe', which had been covered by a net. Once they reached the narrower end, the net was dropped and the birds, trapped.

BELOW
The 13th century earth-fast timber buildings at Barton Blount were superseded by sturdier timber-framed houses, the supports of which rested on 'padstones'. None have survived, however, and horses now run on the old village site.

WEST BURTON
NOTTINGHAMSHIRE

ABOVE

A map of West Burton in 1865 shows that at that time, only the church remained. Today, even the church has vanished, yet a few gravestones from the churchyard still remain.

BELOW

The depopulation of West Burton seems to have occurred under the land-lordship of Allan Johnson, Esq., continuing, until 1818, under his successor George Moody, Esq.

Today, West Burton is a 2,000-megawatt coal-fired power station that stands on a 165-hectare (410-acre) site in north Nottinghamshire. Yet in the shadow of its immense concrete cooling towers lie the earthworks of a deserted medieval village. West Burton is situated alongside a tidal stretch of the River Trent, where Kingfishers and cormorants abound, while amid the reed beds, sparrow hawks and long-eared owls eye their prey. Records show that on 22 November 1271, Henry III (1207–72) granted a weekly Friday Market and annual Whitsunday fair to Simon Preston, Lord of the Manor of West Burton. In 1334, the village paid a fairly respectable contribution of over £46 to the Lay Subsidy, and in 1434 its tax quota was considered high. It weathered both the Black Death and the subsequent reorganization of rural areas, as can be seen from a map of 1750 that shows a church and 15 houses. Yet just 40 years later, the number of houses had dropped to just seven or eight, inhabited by around 45 people.

Industry expands as agriculture declines

From the mid-18th century, as industrial towns and villages expanded, communities that relied solely on agriculture went into protracted and severe decline. It has been calculated that no fewer than 150 parishes in Nottinghamshire contracted during that period, with one village, West Burton, becoming totally deserted. Areas that had held 23 percent of the population in 1831 contained just six percent by 1931. A map drawn in 1895 shows that there was literally nothing left at West Burton except for the church, which was demolished shortly afterwards. In the 1950s, Professor Maurice Beresford wrote that the graves in the churchyard were said to be 'yawning' open, and that the streets of the village could be seen on the banks of the Trent.

A series of oval depressions among the earthworks at the southern end of the site have been interpreted as ponds, and may represent a fishery, possibly the one that was recorded in the Domesday Book. Three rectangular tofts line up in the north-eastern corner of the site, two of which display the foundations of medieval buildings at their eastern ends. A lane passes along their western edge. Further south, two more tofts abut the main hollow-way of the village, and another two, showing faint signs of having once supported structures, can be seen north-west of the site of the church. Two well-defined building-platforms are situated just north

of the southernmost hollow-way. Elsewhere on the site, erosion has revealed areas of dressed stone, thought to be the foundations of a medieval homestead. Fragments of the village's open fields, in the form of patches of ridge and furrow, can still be seen in a field to the south-west of Low Farm, which also contains a large irregular pond.

Between 1994 and 1996, the Trent and Peak Archaeological Unit carried out the 'Nottinghamshire Village Earthwork Survey'. When it was completed, 329 settlement-related earthworks had been recorded – a considerable advance on the 27 shrunken or deserted settlements reported by Beresford in 1954. However, the scope of the later study was much wider, including a variety of settlements, from single house-platforms to the large abandoned earthworks around shrunken villages or towns.

After the Second World War, power stations producing clean and relatively cheap electricity were built along the banks of the Trent, giving a much-needed boost to the county's coal industry. Their distinctive cooling towers dominate the downstream stretch of the river. However, new gas-powered stations might mean that these giant landmarks disappear before too much longer. If this is the case, their remnants will add a new set of earthworks to the story of West Burton.

ABOVE

Cooling towers now dominate the landscape, looming over what was once the thriving village of West Burton.

THE NORTHERN COUNTIES

Frequently, in the north, industrialization and urbanization have erased all traces of the missing medieval villages that we seek. The same powerful processes are often at the root of similarly painful, yet far more modern desertions. Whether it be the thirst of great towns and cities demanding that new reservoirs flood ancient valley settlements and inundate the homes of peasant and poet alike; or the hardship in upland communities where the icy driving force of natural torrents was superseded by the scalding motive power of steam; or simply the weary miner's abandonment of an exhausted pit, the toll in human suffering remains a heavy one.

Centuries earlier, many of the northernmost villages in the region had succumbed to the torch during deadly border raids inflicted by the Scots. Elsewhere, land still smouldering from Norman retribution learned destruction was just as likely to come quietly in the form of zealous monastic orders, whose search for perfect isolation alongside vast consolidated commercial farms saw even those most deserving of charity turned out of their homes.

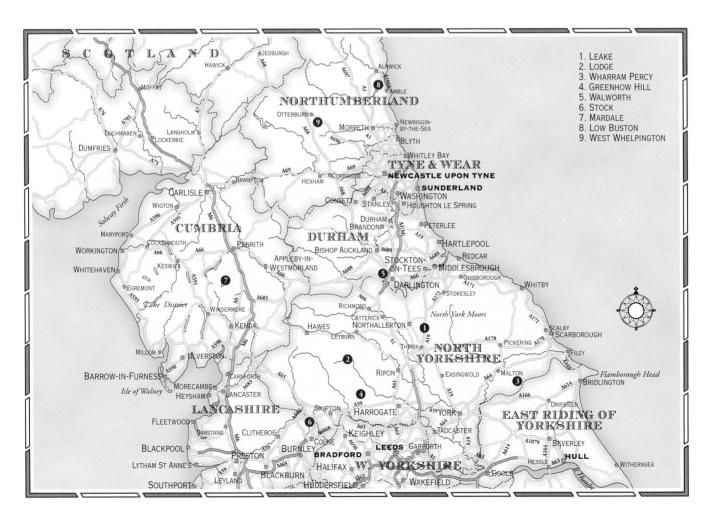

1. LEAKE
2. LODGE
3. WHARRAM PERCY
4. GREENHOW HILL
5. WALWORTH
6. STOCK
7. MARDALE
8. LOW BUSTON
9. WEST WHELPINGTON

LEAKE
YORKSHIRE

PREVIOUS PAGE
The industrial relics and crumbling cottages of Greenhow Hill, Yorkshire, are gradually giving way to a prosperous and attractively restored settlement.

By some accounts, the North Riding settlement of Leake was a town and not a village. Estimates of a peak population somewhere in the region 1,500 inhabitants may turn out to be something of an exaggeration, but one look at the fine Norman church of St Mary should be enough to persuade most people that somewhere in its history, Leake must have been a very busy village indeed.

Village massacres

In 1852, a mass grave was discovered. This was apparently not as big a shock to local people as one might have expected it to be. The story of the massacre of the villagers by James 'the Black' (or 'good' as he was known in Scotland) Douglas (1265–1330) had long been told. The killings were said to have occurred in 1318, when Douglas, an ally of Robert the Bruce, was on his way back to Scotland after burning down the city of York, just 8km

(5 miles) away. If the story is true, it might not have been the first time that the village had encountered bloodshed on such a massive scale. Another local legend tells of a conflict between local Saxons and incoming Danish settlers. In the ensuing violence, it was said that a great many Danes perished. One version of the story has the Saxon women rising up against their Danish oppressors in anguished retaliation for the slaughter of their menfolk during the invasion. It may be significant, or it could just be coincidence, but the pit of bones was uncovered close to a track known as Danes Lane. Of course, an alternative explanation for death on such a scale was plague.

However, for a village to be sacked and not resettled was rare, while total annihilation as a result of pestilence was just as uncommon. Yet Leake was unquestionably depopulated at some point, and it is very tempting to view the mass grave as a clue. St Mary's church tells of a village population after the Danes, and although a Saxon uprising might explain the pit of bones, it does not explain the settlement's desertion. This seems to have occurred in the 14th century, after a period of expansion and prosperity that saw some significant enhancement of the fabric of the church.

There are many possible explanations for the abandonment of Leake – land exhaustion and the migration of the labour force following the social restructuring that occurred in the wake of the Black Death are both plausible. However, it seems curious that Leake was deserted at a time when nearby villages, such as Borrowby, were expanding. One cannot help but wonder if they grew larger at Leake's expense. As the old village declined, and its timber houses rotted and fell, the church became isolated in its road-side position. Today, even the earthworks that once surrounded the church and the turf-covered banks of the old crofts have all but vanished, having been 'comprehensively levelled' by 'modern agricultural activity', according to Beresford. As a result, there is little to see apart from the church, and the site has not been designated as an ancient monument. Leake Hall was built in the 17th century, and its appearance so late in the history of the village absolves it from any charges of depopulation through emparking.

Bishop's rest

While the village may have vanished, the parish of Leake-with-Kepwick lived on. After the Dissolution of the Monasteries in the 16th century, St Mary's Church even acquired a bell and some bench ends from defunct religious institutions. The house opposite the church gates, which was superseded by the present farm building, belonged to the Bishop of Durham, as the gift of the church was with the Cathedral there. Lying at the edge of the North Yorkshire Moors, halfway between York and Durham, Leake acted as an overnight stop for the traveling bishop. Yet church and Hall have remained the only constant companions. By 1901, the population of Leake was enumerated as just two.

OPPOSITE TOP
Carved into the wall to the right of the entrance to the church is a medieval representation of some sort of creature.

OPPOSITE BOTTOM
Although the church is Norman in date, a Saxon cross has been built into the west wall of the tower.

BELOW
The Norman church of St Mary the Virgin once served a thriving and populous site consisting of around 1,500 souls.

LODGE
YORKSHIRE

ABOVE

Fragments of dwellings are still visible at Lodge today, as in this example of a cottage window lintel.

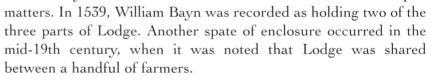

"LODGE, a hamlet in the township of Upper Stonebeck, and parish of Kirkbymalzeard; 6 miles from Kettlewell."

WHITE'S TRADE DIRECTORY FOR THE NORTH RIDING OF YORKSHIRE, 1822

In the local trade directory of 1822, Lodge merits only a brief entry, for there was little to say. This was no centre of commerce. Lodge was a grouping of five farmsteads, the occupants of which were engaged in the herding of cattle and the shepherding of sheep across the slopes of Nidderdale in the valley between Carlton and Ridge moors. Just below Dead Man's Hill, apparently so called because a murdered drover was once discovered there, a crease in the valley afforded some meagre protection from the often bitterly cold prevailing winds that sweep across this otherwise exposed landscape. Within this geological fold were huddled the dwellings of lonely, isolated Lodge.

A bleak setting

By the 13th century, the granges of Bylands and Fountains abbeys dominated the farming landscape of the area, not least because it was their custom to plant fast-growing sycamore trees as windbreaks. The abbots had acquired control of the entire chase of Nidderdale and divided it between them. For the isolated hill farmers, however, a change in lordship probably mattered less than the state of the weather and the health of their animals. They are likely to have been hired by the abbeys as shepherds, and, in addition to the care of their flocks, other duties may have involved transporting fleeces back to the abbey precincts.

As with all farming communities, the pattern of their lives was dictated by the changing seasons. In addition, there were only certain times of the year when the roads across the moorland were easily passable. Heavy snows fell on these uplands in winter, and the roads were really only suitable for travel by horse or on foot. Goods and cattle were moved at regular times, which explains how the drover's murderer might have been able to predict his appearance. Land division and the fragmentation of holdings were rife among the properties of both abbeys, and the 16th-century Dissolution of the Monasteries could not have helped matters. In 1539, William Bayn was recorded as holding two of the three parts of Lodge. Another spate of enclosure occurred in the mid-19th century, when it was noted that Lodge was shared between a handful of farmers.

Industrial impact

By 1874, the local travelling Wesleyan minister reported just 12 members in his congregation at Lodge. Farming on the moorland margins had been in retreat for some time, and settlement populations declined as a consequence. This drift coincided with the Bradford Water Company's aim to ensure that the thriving industrial town never had to go short of water. As a result, teams of engineers were sent out in search of suitable sites for the construction of reservoirs.

An area at the top of the Nidd Valley was chosen, and an Act of 1880 authorized the construction of three reservoirs. High Woodale, Lodge and Angram were the sites selected, and work soon began on the 50-km (31-mile) aqueduct that would carry the

water to the treatment works at Chellow Heights. By 1913, it was decided that another Act was required to allow the Bradford Corporation (who had taken over the project in 1856) to construct Scar House reservoir. Leases to farms and small-holdings in the affected parts of the valley were purchased or not renewed and it was not long before Lodge was empty.

A modern, model village
As one settlement was abandoned, a model village, financed by the Bradford Corporation, was being occupied. It was built to accommodate the construction workers and their families at Scar House, and was situated on the opposite side of the Nidd valley to Lodge. Scar Village housed

1,250 inhabitants, many enjoying the delights of running water, electric lights and flush toilets for the first time. Shops, a cinema, a concert hall and a hospital were also provided.

Work began on the Scar House Reservoir in 1921, and was completed in 1936. It could hold 1,000 million litres (2,200 million gallons) of water, and covered an area of 70 hectares (172 acres). Lodge itself was not drowned under all this water, but much of the local farmland was submerged. The existence of a village or hamlet at the water's edge was considered too much of a health risk, and Lodge was allowed to decay. For once it is easy to locate the site of the deserted village on the banks of the reservoir – just look for the sycamores.

ABOVE
Just beyond the remains of a cottage door one can see the site of the lost village of Lodge, marked by a stand of Sycamores once planted as windbreaks.

OPPOSITE
Various items of domestic furniture are strewn around the lost village site, yet few of them, even heavy objects such as this cast iron cooking range, remain in situ.

WHARRAM PERCY
YORKSHIRE

Probably the most famous of all deserted medieval village sites, Wharram Percy, on the high chalk Wolds of East Yorkshire, is also one of the most enchanting. Situated on the western side of a steep, dry valley called Deep Dale, the distinctive remains of peasant houses, manor house, millpond and ruined church represent the final chapter in a story of human occupation that stretches back into prehistory.

Traces of Mesolithic, Neolithic and Bronze Age habitation have been identified here, both from the air and through excavations on the ground. A high-status burial dating to the 1st century BC provides the first tangible evidence for a permanent focus of human activity. Later, Iron Age enclosures and trackways were incorporated into a Roman settlement on the site, the boundaries of which were in some places respected, and elsewhere modified by the dispersed Anglo-Saxon farmsteads and hamlets of the 7th to 9th centuries.

Only at some as yet unidentified point in the ensuing three hundred years did a truly nucleated village emerge. When it did, both the pattern of settlement and the name of the village suggest Scandinavian origins (Wharram is thought to derive from an old Scandinavian word meaning 'at the bends'). Its rectangular tofts and regular layout hint at a strong element of planning, possibly carried out in multiple phases, and guided by the much earlier field boundaries.

By Domesday, 'Warron', as it was recorded, was in the hands of the King, and comprised 8 carucates of land divided into two manors, with a further 1 carucate designated 'sokeland' of the nearby manor of Wharram le Street. Documentary evidence suggests the situation had changed little by 1242, by which time the Chamberlain family had become the major landowners at West Wharram, as it was then known. As well, one William de Percy had held land there from 1176, and by 1254, one Peter de Percy had managed to acquire the rights to the entire village. It would take nearly 40 years more for the family name to be added to that of the village, and even then it apparently took some time to catch on. A century later, the Percys had exchanged their manor at Wharram for one closer to their main seats in Northumberland, and the Hilton family of Hylton Castle, near Sunderland, became the village's next and final owners.

By the early 14th century, the once-prosperous village was clearly in a state of decline, with as much as two thirds of its land uncultivated. Its two water mills lay idle, and a number of holdings stood vacant. There were still, however, 18 inhabited households in 1323, including the parsonage and manor house. Then, in 1349, the Black Death cut the population from around 67 to 45. By 1368, the village seems to have rallied, with as many as 30 houses occupied; one of the mills not only operational once more but profitably so; both the millponds generating an income from fishing, and all of the land that had been left uncultivated in 1323 now productive. It was to prove a relatively short-lived recovery, however. A century later, the Manor House was in such a poor state of repair that it was considered worthless, and although the village struggled on, with the mill still operational and 16 occupied houses in 1458, soon the population decreased sharply. Growth in the textile industry brought about a significant increase in the demand for wool, which encouraged many landlords to turn arable land over to pasture — and the peasant farmers out of their homes.

RIGHT
Excavated from c.1950-1990, the outline of this longhouse has been left sketched on the ground.

BELOW
Their homes demolished for sheep pasturage, the villagers finally abandoned medieval Wharram Percy in the early 16th century.

GREENHOW HILL
YORKSHIRE

ABOVE
The squat-towered church of St Mary at the old lead mining village of Greenhow Hill.

Greenhow is a village that was almost lost. During the 1970s, many of the short rows of dark millstone grit lead miners' cottages were showing serious signs of decay, and some of the scattered farmsteads were derelict. With little in the way of local employment once the mines were closed, and with few families actively engaged in farming any longer, the village's young inhabitants looked for better opportunities in places such as Harrogate, Skipton or Leeds. The older folk, meanwhile, sought comfortable retirement at a lower altitude in the pleasant small town of Pateley Bridge, which is just 6.5km (4 miles) down the dale, and sheltered from the worst of the harsh north winds that scour exposed Greenhow.

Monks and miners

Situated midway between Wharfedale and Nidderdale, and about 400m (1,300 feet) above sea level, the village was first conceived in the early 17th century to house the workers at the local lead mines – lead had been mined in the vicinity since Roman times. Later the land around Greenhow became part of the Fountains Abbey estate. A small, two-roomed cottage was built by the side of the main track at the edge of Craven Moor, within which two monks lived. The monks were tasked with providing care for passing travellers, tending the abbey's flock and, no doubt, guarding against the theft of lead ore. This early part of the settlement at Greenhow was known as Kell or Keld Houses.

Following the dissolution of the monasteries in the 1530s, the buildings and some of the lands of the Fountains Estate were acquired by Sir Richard Gresham, although they were sold to the ambitious Stephen Proctor in 1597. Proctor's father, Thomas, was a successful entrepreneur who had patented a process for smelting iron and lead using a mixture of coal, charcoal and peat, a technique his son was keen to exploit. In 1613 the Court of Chancery granted Sir Stephen Proctor (he had been knighted in 1604) the right to erect a number of cottages near his lead mines at Greenhow, complete with common grazing rights for draught oxen and horses. These buildings also housed the mineral workers who worked in the limestone quarry, and were primarily intended to do away with the hard climb up the dale each day.

Although the local seams were narrow, the price of lead was such that at first the Greenhow mines were very successful. The settlement gradually expanded eastwards from Keld, and into the dip between the hills of Greenhow and Coldstone. Most of the miners were also part-time small-holders, and the community was fairly self-sufficient. In addition to an Anglican church, there were also two

BELOW
Recently renovated cottages at Greenhow Hill. After a steady period of decline, interest in the village picked up in the 1980s, and the village is now a popular place to live.

Wesleyan Methodist chapels – John Wesley himself is said to have preached at one of them – and a Congregational chapel. The Post Office and general store dated back to the mid-19th century, and the community had its own school.

But by the 1880s, with most of the wider seams played out and the arrival of cheap imported lead from countries such as Spain, the mines were no longer profitable. The miners that remained subsisted on occasional farm work, road repairing and some limited small-scale mining. There was a short-lived revival in the early 20th century when, encouraged by rising lead prices, a man by the name of Harald Bruff proposed reopening some of the old mines to extract lead and fluorspar. But although the Greenhaugh Mining Company was eventually registered in 1915, the outbreak of the Great War, as well as numerous technical difficulties, meant that the venture was only moderately successful. All mining operations had ceased by the 1930s. Limestone continued to be extracted, however, and was used in the construction of several local roads. Some quarrying goes on at Greenhow to this day.

Home for the holidays

With the village's population in serious decline, many of its houses stood empty and derelict. Prospects for the village looked bleak. However, in the 1980s, a new interest in Greenhow Hill emerged, and many of the old cottages were bought and refurbished as weekend homes. Those too far gone to save were demolished, with new properties constructed in their place. Suddenly, Greenhow Hill became a desirable place to live and, back from the brink of extinction, it is now a popular commuter village. A combination of low property prices and breathtaking scenery has attracted resettlement, yet the landscape still bears the scars of the extraction industry. It is littered with rusted pit gear and the ruins of old engine houses – slowly decaying reminders of a proud and industrious past.

ABOVE
The remains of an arch kiln at the Providence Smelt Mill. Both iron and lead were smelted at Greenhow Hill.

WALWORTH
COUNTY DURHAM

ABOVE
An aerial view of the deserted settlement site, taken 19 November 1974.

Walworth has Saxon origins, yet it did not survive past the 16th century. Its late-12th-century chapel decayed to the point that it was used both as a granary and to house pigs. Modern farm buildings now occupy the village green, incorporating the parts of the chapel that still stand, while a road and the gardens of a large country hotel beyond encroach on the old village's outlying fields to the south.

BELOW LEFT
A farmhouse now stands on the former village green, with the earthworks of the deserted settlement all around. Walworth Castle, a mansion built c1600, and now a hotel, can also be seen.

View from above
Walworth is a village best appreciated from the air, for then the full layout of the planned settlement that was neatly arranged around its square green can be seen with utter clarity. While the earthworks are generally well preserved under permanent pasture, centuries of activity have abraded their profiles. There is also one quite puzzling feature of the village that is only really noticeable from the air. Large expanses of ridge and furrow can be seen extending northwards from the end of the row of crofts, but from the north-eastern corner of the main village site stretches a long, narrow extension, corrugated with ridge and furrow and lined with faint traces of further crofts. It has been suggested that this was an earlier manifestation of the village, which was subsequently reorganized around the green, or that, conversely, it represents a later expansion of the village.

BELOW RIGHT
King James VI of Scotland is said to have been a visitor at the Walworth manor house.

Castle and chapel
To the south lies Walworth Castle, which is now a hotel. Much of the present building dates from the 16th century, but a handful of older sections may have been incorporated from the ruins of a castle that once stood on the site. Built by Thomas Jennison, who purchased the estate in 1579, the medieval castle-like manor house is said to have played host to King

JAMES VI.

James VI of Scotland (1566–1625) as he made his way to London for his coronation as James I of England in 1603. If this is the case, then it is likely that James saw something of the village of Walworth, although just 23 years later there are reports of it being in a state of decay. Two and a half centuries on, only the earthworks surrounding the ruined Norman chapel could be seen.

Walworth's chapel was built in about 1180, some 30 years after the castle and village were constructed by the Hansard family. A Saxon settlement called 'Waleberge' (or 'settlement of the Welsh') had existed there before the Norman Conquest, its name referring to the ancient Britons who migrated to the margins of their territories when the Saxon settlers arrived and took over.

There is a local legend that the village was wasted by Malcolm IV of Scotland as he passed along the River Tees, which flows just 4km (2½ miles) to the south. The river formed the border between England and Scotland in the early 12th century. If true, it may have been this catastrophe that cleared the way for the planned settlement. Walworth remained in the hands of the Hansard family until 1579, when it was purchased by Thomas Jenison, Auditor General of Ireland, whose descendents held the manor for the next 180 years. Perhaps the change of ownership in the late-16th century brought with it new farming policies, and these may have contributed to the ultimate decay of the village.

Three sides of the central green still show the rectangular boundaries of the medieval longhouses. These are backed by long crofts, which have scooped yards and gardens that once fronted the green. Often up to 33m (100 feet) long and 12m (40 feet) wide, several of the longhouses show obviously sub-divided interiors. Stock enclosures are also evident, as are a number of hollow-ways, one of which is 15m (50 feet) wide and enters the village at its the north-eastern corner, while a large rectangular pinfold or stack-stand lies on the green's western edge.

Today, the 'lost' village of Walworth is on private property, but it can be viewed from the road.

ABOVE
Longhouses once lay adjacent to the central green, with their crofts behind. Could these stones represent their remains?

STOCK
LANCASHIRE

ABOVE
Earthworks running southwards downhill at the village site.

BELOW
The Stock Beck runs through the well-defined village remains.

Most of the detailed studies about deserted medieval settlements have concentrated on nucleated villages of the type found in the Midlands. This has meant that counties such as Cumbria, Cheshire and Lancashire, where a different settlement agenda was in operation, have received far less attention. Medieval Lancashire was a county of dispersed farmsteads and hamlets. In east Lancashire in particular, the subsequent development of land has obscured much of the medieval settlement pattern. Elsewhere in the county, the irregular and dispersed nature of the villages make desertions difficult to identify. Consequently, the list of deserted medieval villages in Lancashire is rather a short one; about 40 villages have been named, nearly a third of them falling within the Ribble Valley.

Easington

No excavations on the scale of Wharram Percy in Yorkshire (see pages 150–151) have been carried out in Lancashire. In 1975, however, members of the Pendle Archaeological Group worked on a site at Manor House Farm in the Ribble Valley. Every summer for 12 years they searched for the lost village of Easington, and did make some discoveries. But did they find Easington? The jury remains out on that point.

A positive identification

One Lancashire deserted medieval settlement that has been positively identified, however, is Stock. An estate plan of 1717 clearly shows a blank area among fields that is helpfully labelled 'Stock Towne', and aerial photographs have revealed the layout of the village's extensive earthworks. These images emphasize that the buried remains of this particular village are unusual even for Lancashire. Stock has no discernible plan; instead it appears to have developed in a piecemeal fashion around an irregular central field that has a hollow-way leading to it. Tofts, crofts, paddocks and stock enclosures are all suggested by the prominent earthworks, along with part of an associated medieval open field system. Less common are the horseshoe-shaped earthworks, which have been interpreted as lime kilns, while at Stock Green there is a series of earthworks that may represent the manor house.

The origins of the settlement at Stock are unknown (although numerous indications of

Roman activity have been found in the vicinity) and little has been written about its history. We are therefore heavily dependent on the physical evidence at the site itself, but however distinct the earthworks may be, the village remains something of a puzzle. Recorded as 'Stoche' in the Domesday Book, the name of the settlement suggests that it originated as an outlying subsidiary settlement, and as such may never have reached any significant size, although the 'classic' medieval earthworks extending across the site have often been cited as evidence for a period of prosperity prior to extreme shrinkage in the aftermath of the Black Death. Indeed, the aforementioned estate plan of 1717 records just five distinct properties at Stock, yet, curiously, on a subsequent plan dated 1796, these had been joined by nine more.

This growth can be explained by the duel economy of farming and weaving known to have been in operation in the village at that time. Improvements in agrarian technology during the latter half of the 18th century coincided with increased mechanization of all aspects of the cloth making process – except in the area of weaving. Consequently, Stock's farmers and cottage industry handloom weavers prospered. Yet by the middle of the 19th century, agricultural depression, together with the widespread use of factory-based power-looms, brought about a reversal in the village's fortunes that may have encouraged its inhabitants to seek employment, and ultimately, homes in nearby Barnoldswick, thus initiating a drift. Today, Stock has been reduced to just five properties once more.

For the time being, Stock is classified as a deserted medieval settlement, and its earthworks are protected as a Scheduled Ancient Monument, even though it is possible that much of the site can be dated to the 18th and 19th centuries.

MARDALE (HAWESWATER)
CUMBRIA

ABOVE
In times of drought, the level of the reservoir drops, and gradually the lost village of Mardale reappears.

BELOW
The walls of stone-built field enclosures can be seen disappearing into the water at the edge of the reservoir.

In the late 1930s, explosions echoed down the Mardale Valley. It was the terrible sound of the Territorial Army dynamiting the old stone cottages of Mardale Green. Later, the noise of demolition was replaced by the rhythmic strike of the woodsman's axe, as the six 800-year-old yews flanking Holy Trinity Church were felled. As the old village was systematically dismantled, the stones of the medieval church were removed and the graves in the churchyard opened, their 100 occupants removed for reburial to Shap, some 18km (11 miles) away.

The villagers had protested long and hard against the destruction of their homes and community, and other voices from far and wide had given their support, but the letters and petitions were ultimately all in vain. Years had passed since last orders were called for the final time in the centuries-old Dun Bull pub, while 18 August 1935 saw the very last service to be held at Holy Trinity Church – 80 people crowded into the tiny place of worship and hundreds more gathered outside. On that occasion, the Reverend Barham had been too distressed to enter the old building where his wind-up gramophone had scratched out the hymns for service after service, year after year. Among the congregation that day were people from the new

model village of Burnbanks, welcomed by the local folk even though the men among them were engaged in work that would ultimately lead to the annihilation of Mardale Green and the tiny community of Measands. The sheep and dairy farming settlements of one of Westmorland's most picturesque valleys were to be drowned to form a reservoir for Manchester and the urban conurbations of the north-east of England. The land had been taken by a compulsory purchase order that was approved by an Act of Parliament in 1919, just after the end of the Great War. The Mardale Beck, beside which the village had been established in medieval times (or perhaps even earlier), was to be dammed to create Haweswater, one of the largest of Cumbria's lakes. The 'navvies' from Burnbanks would take the stones of Holy Trinity to construct the draw off tower for the dam, and glass from the church windows was to glaze the reservoir tower. The construction of the concrete dam was considered an engineering marvel of its time, as it was the first hollow buttress dam in the world. At 470 m (1,550 feet) wide and 36 m (120 feet) high it would have the capacity to hold 85 billion litres (18.6 billion gallons) of water. However, work on the Manchester Corporation's dam was delayed. The Great Depression of the 1930s placed financial constraints on the project, and when construction finally got underway in 1934, it was interrupted by the Second World War. In fact, Haweswater Dam was not fully completed until 1955.

Originally, Mardale had contained two small natural lakes, High Water and Low Water. When the dam was finally plugged in 1941, their levels began to rise. Not everyone was impressed with the results, however. Alfred Wainwright, famous for his *Pictorial Guides to the Lakeland Fells*, bemoaned the 'clumsy hands' that had wrought the 'aggressively ugly' tidemark of the new lake.

After the war, with their work now at an end, the people of Burnbanks began to drift away. Some of the village's 66 houses were demolished, but a few remained and a campaign was started to save them.

The village resurfaces

In 1995, the village of Mardale returned. A serious drought caused the level of the reservoir to drop to such an extent that it became possible once more to wander the lanes of Mardale Green and walk across the old Chapel Bridge. However, when word spread, hoards of souvenir hunters jostled with former residents, grabbing mementoes from the churchyard and ripping stones from the side of the bridge. In the end, the police were forced to close the narrow road along the edge of the lake. Mardale continues to make the occasional reappearance at times of low rainfall, but the main draw today is the news that the Haweswater Valley is the only place in England where golden eagles nest.

ABOVE
The ruined remains of a drowned cottage that once stood within the lost village of Mardale.

LOW BUSTON
NORTHUMBERLAND

North of Hadrian's Wall, in the parish of Warkworth, the remains of the village of Low Buston can be found. Little more than a hamlet, it was first documented in 1242. Yet having survived border raids and pestilence, it fell into disuse towards the end of the 18th century. From about 1774, the buildings in the village were either pulled down or allowed to decay.

Northumberland is not renowned for its vast fields of swaying corn, and so it is often assumed that any apparent immunity to depopulation must be due to a long and widespread predominance of pastoral farming and dispersed settlements. No commissioners from the 1517 inquiry into the abuse of enclosure even ventured to the county. But Northumberland is rich in nucleated settlements, and these were protected against enclosure largely because of their adopted system of mixed arable and pastoral agriculture. Yet issues relating to border tenure during the reign of Elizabeth I (1533–1603), and matters arising from emparking a century or so later, resulted in a measure of depopulation and failure of communities.

Surprisingly, border warfare in the early Middle Ages and the depredatory raids of the 'reivers' (Scots who raided for cattle and sheep) until the 17th century were not major causes of desertion. It was not uncommon for settlements north of Hadrian's Wall to undergo several reconstructions, and if the original site was a good one, then it would not go uninhabited for long.

Nucleated villages in Northumberland were smaller than their counterparts in the Midlands, no doubt reflecting the lower quality and productivity of the soil, although vast tracts of moorland pasture certainly mitigated the impact of these disadvantages. The average number of taxpayers in the Coquetdale ward, in which Low Buston lies, was just 31. Although figures are not available, it is highly unlikely that there were ever that many taxpayers in Low Buston, which seems to have been a village verging on a hamlet.

Situated on a ridge overlooking a small stream known as the Tylee Burn, which tumbles down the slope to the Coquetdale River and the harbour at Warkworth, the ancient manor house of Low Buston would have dominated the village site occupying the eastern slope below. The exact location of the old manor house has not been traced, but the earthworks of the village can be easily seen in a large pasture field to the east of Low Buston Hall.

A sunken trackway, probably representing the settlement's main street, runs through the centre of the site before turning to join the modern road in the south. Along the west side of this track, an ancient boundary marks the eastern edge of the north field's ridge and furrow. Several other hollow-ways criss-cross the site, while great banks of earth some 3m (10 feet) wide and just 0.5m (1½ feet) tall define rectangular enclosures that may once have been small fields. There are also a number of smaller enclosures containing sunken rectangular features

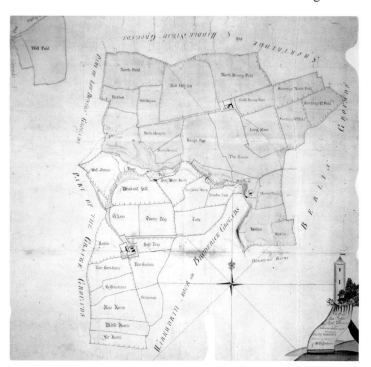

that appear to be the remaining vestiges of buildings.

Elusive evidence

A 6m (20 foot) by 4m (13 foot) structure, built with roughly dressed freestone and standing to a height of 1 m (3 feet) is all that remains of the old village well house. The chapel, however, has proved more elusive. Anecdotal evidence suggests that a granary situated at the upslope end of the settlement occupied the site, but no physical evidence to support this has yet been located.

It may simply have been the case that small-scale park landscaping was carried out when a new hall was built to replace the old medieval manor house, but by the end of the 18th century, the tiny village of Low Buston had become mere undulations in the grounds of a fine country residence.

ABOVE
A stream on the east side of the site. Alongside it can be seen what is perhaps the last remaining piece of wall from the old village of Low Buston.

WEST WHELPINGTON

NORTHUMBERLAND

ABOVE

Ridge and furrow strip patterns are clearly visible in the fields surrounding the lost village site.

BELOW

An aerial view of what was West Whelpington. The quarrying activity that has destroyed much of the site can be seen in this photograph.

If deserted medieval village sites are acknowledged to be an excellent way of tracing the development of settlements and the various forms taken by ordinary buildings without all the confusion of modern disturbance, then West Whelpington is particularly useful. This is a settlement that was not finally depopulated until about 1720, and despite modification of the site in the late-16th and early-17th centuries, it is still possible to trace the transition from medieval to post-medieval building practices as applied to peasants' houses, few of which have survived to the present day.

In the mid-1960s, fears grew that this rare relic of a post-medieval community was going to be swept away entirely. From 1937, quarrying of the whinstone outcrop on which the village was constructed ate away at the site at such a rate that by the summer of 1965 it was feared that it would be totally destroyed within another 20 years. Thankfully, however, extraction ceased in 1971, and the quarry is now leased to the police, who use it as a shooting range. On days when the red flag is not flying, it is still possible to climb the steep path around the rim of the quarry and walk up onto a grassy plateau that undulates with the well-defined earthworks of hollow-ways and house-platforms.

A high and unsteady site

West Whelpington lies north of Hadrian's Wall, and is over 200m (700 feet) above sea level. In 1827, John Hodgson, one of England's greatest county historians and, coincidentally, vicar of Whelpington Parish, was moved to comment that the climate was 'too high and unsteady to allow much of it to be advantageously employed in agriculture'. Instead, much of the land was used for keeping sheep or dairy cattle. Hodgson also tells how just 50 years earlier, 'the people of this place had so little employment about home that many of them went annually into Lincolnshire during the corn-harvest to earn a subsistence during the winter; but they very generally, in addition to their wages, brought back with them the ague, which often became infectious, and spread through the whole of the families into which it was introduced.'

Life in the village was clearly challenging. Even so, documents from the 12th century indicate that the settlement was flourishing, and an assessment for the Lay Subsidy tax of 1296 indicates that, although not as large or as prosperous as its near neighbour, Kirkwhelpington, the community was still

doing reasonably well. No doubt the Scottish border wars (*c.*1300-1550) had a detrimental effect, but even so, the 'Order of the Watchers upon the Middle Marches', which was laid down in the post-war Border Laws of 1552, required that 'From West-Whelpington to Raye, [was] to be watched with four Men nightly of the Inhabitors of West-Whelpington and Ray; Setters and Searchers William Elsden and John Rochester'. This suggests that it was still a village of some note at that point in time.

The parish of Whelpington was large, and included 10 townships. Taking into consideration the usual under-recording that occurred, parish registers are a poor source from which to try and judge the relative strengths and weaknesses of the constituent parts of such a large area. However, they are useful in that they contain the last mention of West Whelpington – it came on the 24 August 1719, and marked the baptism of Anne, daughter of Henry Crenstone.

Deliberate destruction

That the final depopulation of the village was a deliberate act is certain, but the motives behind it are somewhat less clear. Even the identity of the agent of depopulation has not been determined, though likely candidates are Thomas Stott or his brother, Joseph. Although they behaved very much like lords of the manor, the Stotts did not own West Whelpington; they were the long-time tenants of the Millbank family of Thorpe Perrow, in Yorkshire. But by the 1720s, they had leased the entire estate, and seemed to be able to do as they pleased. In 1721, a Stott is said to have evicted the last 15 inhabitants of the village. Later commentators viewed this act as yet another depopulation in favour of sheep, but it is also possible that it may have stemmed from the desire to create more efficient arable farming. Cornhills, one of the larger farms on the estate, was first recorded in 1689, its name perhaps giving some clue as to where the emphasis in husbandry practises lay.

ABOVE
This long, thin rectangular earthwork may represent the foundations of a chapel.

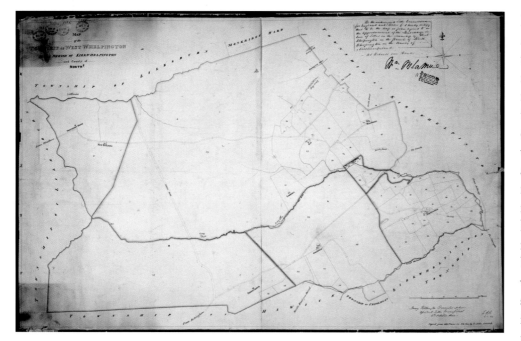

ABOVE

A Whelpington Parish map from 1844.

OPPOSITE

The settlement at West Whelpington went through several phases of development and re-development. These phases were only unravelled when the site was excavated in the 1960s by Michael G. Jarrett.

Certainly the mid-18th century population of West Whelpington – five men and one boy – was larger than necessary if the site had been put over to pasture. Perhaps developments at West Whelpington were influenced by those at nearby Kirkwhelpington, where Sir Walter Calverley Blackett had successfully fashioned a model agricultural estate from a motley collection of unfenced crofts, pastures, moors and fells. At any rate, there is no trace of West Whelpington on Andrew Armstrong's county map of 1769, although Greenwood's map, produced in 1828, does show the former location of the village, perhaps as a result of Hodgson's work.

Hodgson viewed the ruins before the extensive stone robbing of the late-19th century, which saw most of the houses of West Whelpington recycled into field boundary walls. He described the village as being 'of an oblong form, about 440 yards [400m] long', and said that it 'consisted of two rows of houses inclosing [sic] a large town green'. Hodgson also noted a stone circle, which he took to be a cock-pit (although it was more likely an animal pen), and a pele tower, of which subsequent excavations have found no trace. In the 1960s, an archaeological investigation by Michael G. Jarrett brought to light elements of West Whelpington that could not be understood from a perusal of the surface. For the village seems to have been rebuilt more than once.

Phases of occupation

At least three distinct phases of occupation have been identified, each with a markedly different plan. Oddly, there is no evidence of any Saxon settlement on the site, although 'Whelpington' has a distinctly Saxon ring to it. Much of what is visible today are the remains of a 17th-century modification of a late-medieval village built atop an early medieval settlement. Phase one seems to have ended with a series of fires, which may have been connected with the border raids during the Anglo-Scots wars of the 1300s. The 19 or so scattered homesteads were replaced by four planned rows of longhouses that ranged around the sides of the rectangular central green. By the end of this second phase of building, there were around 28 larger properties, along with eight or so smaller cottages. Yet shrinkage is apparent almost immediately. The western section of the village was abandoned, and a boundary was built across the green to enable the villagers to turn the disused area over to pasture. In the 17th century, the terraces were modified to create around 13 separate farmsteads, with the small crofts and enclosures amalgamated into larger holdings. It seems that before the final depopulation occurred, at least three of these small-holdings were abandoned, as was the forge. Once the last villagers had been evicted, the land was divided between just four large farms.

The understanding of transitions in the use of building materials, building orientation and spatial arrangement from the early medieval period through to the early 18th-century has been greatly enhanced by the excavations at West Whelpington. But perhaps the last words on the subject should be left to Hodgson, who not only commented on the distinct ruins and 'beautiful verdure' of the site, but also considered West Whelpington 'one of the numerous places in the north where a long line of ancient tenantry had toiled and gambolled; but were forced, by a new order of things, to quit the only spot on earth that was dear to them.'

CONCLUSION

Why did villages fail? In most cases, those that disappeared were already small and
weak, although even a healthy village might be felled by nature or national emergency.

In the middle years of the 14th century, after the Black Death had struck a country already in crisis, everything changed forever. Land-hunger was replaced by a land-glut almost overnight, and with it went the old order upon which the social structure of society had been based since pre-Conquest times. The customary workforce of large estates, which had performed the annual agricultural tasks on the demesne in return for a dwelling and a small patch of ground, were now too few in number on some manors to cultivate the vast open fields effectively. Wage labour

BELOW: *Remodelling the church to manageable proportions saved neither it nor Covehithe village from coastal erosion.*

became more necessary than ever before, and the post-pestilence labourers knew their market value. Landowners whose revenue from rents had been severely curtailed by properties lying empty struggled to meet the new demands. The peasantry began to favour task-free leaseholds, and landlords slow to grasp this trend lost out when it came to attracting new tenants to their villages. All that empty land meant that small-holders could enlarge their holdings for little extra expense, and suddenly the old order of custom and obligation was replaced with a new regime of competition and ambition. From a life of little opportunity, there was suddenly potential.

The Great Pestilence itself rarely caused complete depopulation, but it was the catalyst that led to desertion and eviction. It gave choice to people who had never known choice before, and perspectives changed. Under the circumstances, a reorganization of rural resources was inevitable, and like any process of rationalization, there were bound to be casualties. With sheep needing less attention than crops, grain proving less profitable than wool, and with fewer people to feed, the switch from one type of farming to the other was inevitable in many places. Of course, the best arable land remained profitable and was never under serious threat, but elsewhere, with the vast open fields of many villages already unkempt and overgrown, the move to pasture was the only sensible solution to the problems of lack of tenants, lack of labour force and lack of profits. Even so, enclosing the fields to make them suitable for flocks of sheep was an expensive process, and not one likely to have been undertaken lightly. In most cases, it represented a last resort as opposed to a preferred option, and by that time any village that may once have stood in the way had probably been long deserted.

The peak period of depopulation seems to have occurred during the course of the 15th century, and it is no coincidence that these were also the years when the greatest profits could be derived from wool. But by the 16th century, population levels in England had largely recovered, while at the same time the textile industry was experiencing a decline. Some places reverted to arable farming, although the old village sites, now long forgotten, were not resettled, and many were subsequently ploughed. It was around this time that the creation of private parks started to become fashionable amongst the wealthiest members of English society. When the movement reached its peak in the 18th century, the emparker had replaced the sheep-depopulator as the subject of public opprobrium.

While the avaricious sheep depopulator was not a myth, he was probably an exaggeration. Indeed, in most case studies of lost village sites, we see a combination of factors put forward to explain the settlement's demise, including such variables as the nature of tenure and the distance from the nearest market, alongside the usual issues of soil quality and climate. The reasons for depopulation become less complex as we move closer to the present day. In the 20th century, villages were killed more quickly, and it would appear that 'overnight' eviction is largely a modern phenomenon. The Stanford Battle Training areas were evacuated within a matter of weeks during a time of national crisis, for example, while Hallsands was washed out to sea in less than 24 hours due to a combination of natural forces and human arrogance. In each of these cases, there was undoubtedly an element of shock, but once that had worn off most of the relocated villagers seem to have been content with their new and typically improved surroundings. In the case of the battle training areas, only a small minority lost homes that had actually belonged to them, the majority being renting tenants or the occupants of 'tied' properties. Even so, many of the evicted villagers had loved their adopted cottages as if they had owned them. If anything, these events proved that even at the end of the 2nd millennium there was no greater measure of security of tenure than there had been a thousand years earlier, when numerous old Hampshire villages had been swept away to create William I's vast hunting ground, the New Forest.

That there is an altogether uneven spread of depopulation across the country has long been recognized, the largest concentration of lost village sites being found in the Midlands. However, the relatively sparse distribution in the north and west, which was at first attributed solely to the protection afforded by a long tradition of pastoral farming, is now better understood as a problem of identification. Those engaged in animal husbandry had no protection from the engrossing actions of other pastoral farmers. Nor were they immune to the emparker, as the case of Tatton, Cheshire clearly shows. In fact the north of England had suffered some of the earliest known wholescale evictions in the country when, in the 12th and 13th centuries, the great Cistercian monasteries had ensured seclusion by removing those villages deemed too close. Moreover, the later decline of mill and mining industries would bring a fresh new wave of desertions to the area. Much regional variation in the occurrence of lost villages can now be attributed to the level of scholarly attention received by a particular area, and the ease with which a deserted nucleated village can be identified, compared with the more challenging scattered and dispersed settlement patterns of pastoral or wooded counties.

And so the search for the 'lost' village goes on. The list of known sites is always changing, with new ones being added and sites erroneously included, removed. Archaeologists these days rarely get the opportunity for excavation on the scale of Wharram Percy, indeed most are fighting to stay ahead of the developers. Yet momentum is gathering, and perhaps soon a new generation of historical geographers, landscape historians, archaeologists and local enthusiasts will again take up the work so admirably started in the 1950s by Beresford, Hoskins and Hurst, for there is much still to do, and many of our English villages, for the time being at least, remain lost.

BELOW: *The village of Lodge, abandoned to make way for a reservoir, typifies the sacrifice of a village where the needs of the many outweighed the needs of the few.*

ACCESS TO SITES

Below you will find information on access to the sites of the lost villages in this book. Where access to a village site is not possible, this is noted. Beside each site name is an Ordinance Survey Land Ranger reference, as some of the site locations can be difficult to find.

Note: When using a public right of way to cross farmland, please remember to leave gates and all property as you find them, keep to the path and take heed of signs, especially any warning or danger notices. Please keep dogs on a lead and do not take a dog (even on a lead) into a field containing cows and calves. Be sure to take all litter home.

The South West

Tyneham, Dorset
(OS SY881801)
Open during the month of August, most weekends throughout the year and on all public holidays. For further information contact Range Safety Control for the Lulworth Ranges on 01929 462721, ext. 4819.
Danger: Tyneham is a live firing area so do not attempt unauthorized access.

Grimspound, Dartmoor (Devon)
(OS SX705805)
Open all year at any reasonable time.

Hound Tor, Dartmoor (Devon)
(OS SX746788)
Open all year at any reasonable time.

Hallsands, Devon
(OS SX818387)
There is no direct access to the site,
but a viewing platform has been built on the clifftop above the village. At extremely low tide it is sometimes possible to view the village from the beach, although it is now far too dangerous to walk among the ruins.

Merrivale, Dartmoor (Devon)
(OS SX557763)
Open all year at any reasonable time.

Chysauster, Cornwall
(OS SW472350)
Open throughout the summer (check times with English Heritage at www.english-heritage.co.org). Small admission charge.

Trewortha, Cornwall
(OS SX226760)
No access to Trewortha village, but visitors are welcome at the Trewortha Farm Centre (Iron Age reconstruction), Tel: 01566 782207. For access to Tressellern please telephone first.

Stocklinch Ottersey, Somerset
(OS ST386170)
On private land, however a public footpath passes nearby, and the site can be seen from the churchyard of St Mary's.

Imber, Salisbury Plain (Wiltshire)
(OS ST965485)
The roads through the village are usually open during the month of August; also at Easter and Christmas. Before visiting, please contact: Salisbury Plain Training Area, Westdown Camp, Tilshead, Salisbury, Wiltshire SP3 4RS, Tel: 01980 620819. **Danger:** Imber is a live firing area so do not attempt to access the village unless permission has been granted by Range Control.

Lower Ditchford, Gloucestershire
(OS SP227367)
No access to site, however the site can be viewed from a public footpath that runs alongside.

Upton, Gloucestershire
(OS SP150344)
On private land. No access to site.

The South & South East

Northeye, East Sussex
(OS TQ682070)
On private land, however several public footpaths run across the site.

Oxney, Kent
(OS TR353468)
No access to site.

Quarrendon, Buckinghamshire
(**Quarrendon I** OS SP806156;
Quarrendon II OS SP797158;
Quarrendon III OS SP787177)
On private land, however a public footpath crosses the site and passes close to the church ruins.

Hampton Gay, Oxfordshire
(OS SP486165)
On private land, however a public footpath crosses the site.

Nuneham Courtenay, Oxfordshire
(OS SU540981)
On private land. No access to site.

Hartley Mauditt, Hampshire
(OS SU742362)
On private land, however a public footpath passes close to the site.

Colville, Essex
(OS TL553134)

On private land, however a public footpath passes close to the site.

Newtown, Isle of Wight
(OS SZ424904)
Accessible by road and public footpath.

The Eastern Counties

Segenhoe, Bedfordshire
(OS SP981358)
Accessible by public right of way.

Chellington, Bedfordshire
(OS SP961563)
On private land, however a public footpath crosses the site.

Bletsoe North End, Bedfordshire
(OS TL026593)
On private land, however the site can be seen from the road.

Clopton, Cambridgeshire
(OS TL301487)
On private land, however a public footpath passes close to the site.

Covehithe, Suffolk
(OS TM521818)
Accessible by road.

Bawsey, Norfolk
(OS TF657192)
On private land alongside a farm track.

Stanford Battle Training Area, Norfolk
(OS TL868949)
No access without permission from Range Control. **Danger:** The Stanford Battle Training Area is a live firing area so do not attempt to access the villages without an official escort.

Houghton on the Hill, Norfolk (OS TF869053)

Accessible by public right of way. Contact Bob Davey at 01760 440470.

Egmere, Norfolk
(OS TF896373)
Private farmland, however viewing of the village site is allowed at present although you are asked to leave all cars in the lane. **Note:** The church ruins are dangerous.

Godwick, Norfolk
(OS TF902220)
Access permitted under the Countryside Stewardship Scheme.

Gainsthorpe, Lincolnshire
(OS SE954011)
Open all year at any reasonable time.

Brackenborough, Lincolnshire
(OS TF333903)
Access permitted under the Countryside Stewardship Scheme.

Martinsthorpe, Rutland
(OS SK866044)
On private land, however a public footpath passes close to the site.

Central England & the West

Kilpeck, Herefordshire
(OS SO446306)
No access to village site although the church and castle may be visited.

Throckmorton, Worcestershire
(OS SO983494)
Access via public footpath.

Elmley Lovett, Worcestershire
(OS SO865695)
On private land, however a public footpath crosses the site.

Wormleighton, Warwickshire
(OS   SP442540)

On private land, however the village site is visible from a public footpath.

Braunstonbury & Wolfhampcote, Northants
(OS SP529653)
Access via public footpath.

Mallows Cotton, Northants
(OS SP976733)
On private land, however a public footpath crosses the site.

Sulby, Northants
(OS SP654816)
On private land, however a public footpath crosses the site.

Cold Newton, Leicestershire
(OS SK716066)
Accessible by public right of way

Ingarsby, Leicestershire
(OS SK685051)
On private land, however a public footpath crosses the site.

Wychnor, Staffordshire
(OS SK176158)
No access to deserted village site.

Heath, Shropshire
(OS SO557856)
On private land, however a public footpath crosses the site.

Stokesay, Shropshire
(OS SO435815)
Accessible by road. Stokesay Castle is open from April – September. Small admission charge.

Tatton, Cheshire
(OS SJ757813)
Situated within Tatton Park. Open all year.
Check www.tattonpark.org.uk for opening times.

Hungry Bentley & Alkmonton , Derbyshire
(OS SK178386 & SK194376)
No access to Alkmonton. Hungry Bentley is on private land, however a public footpath crosses the site.

Barton Blount, Derbyshire
(OS SK209349)
No access to site.

West Burton, Nottinghamshire
(OS SK799853)
On private land, however a public footpath crosses the site.

The Northern Counties

Leake, Yorkshire
(OS SE433906)
Access to churchyard.

Lodge, Yorkshire
(OS SE049773)
Access via public footpath.

Wharram Percy, Yorkshire
(OS SE858643)
Open all year at any reasonable time.

Greenhow Hill, Yorkshire
(OS SE110639)
Accessible by road and public footpath.

Walworth, Co Durham
(OS NZ231191)
The site is visible from the road. A public footpath passes nearby.

Stock, Lancashire
(OS SD867489)
A public footpath crosses the site.

Mardale (Haweswater), Cumbria
(OS NY475117)
General location accessible by road. Village remains only visible at times of drought.

Low Buston, Northumberland
(OS NU227072)
Private land, however a public footpath crosses the site.

West Whelpington, Northumberland
(OS NY973838)
No access to site without permission from landowners. Enquire at Cornhills Farmhouse. **Danger:** Police firing range. No unauthorized access.

Also:
West Stow Country Park and Anglo Saxon Village
Open year round from 10am-5pm daily. Admission charge.

Weald and Downland Open Air Museum
Open year round (times vary, check www.wealddown.co.uk for details). Admission charge.

Milton Abbas, Dorset,
Easily reached by car, just off the A354.

BIBLIOGRAPHY

General

K. J. Allison, *Deserted Villages*, Macmillan & Co Ltd, 1970.

M. Aston, *Interpreting the Landscape*, Routledge, 1985.

M. W. Beresford, *The Lost Villages of England*, Sutton Publishing Ltd, 1998.
First published by Lutterworth Press, 1954.

History on the Ground, Sutton Publishing Ltd, 1998.
First published by Lutterworth Press, 1957.

M. W. Beresford & J. G. Hurst, *Deserted Medieval Village*, Lutterworth Press, 1971.

C. Dyer, *Everyday Life in Medieval England*, Hambledon & London Ltd, 2000.

C. Lewis, P. Mitchell-Fox & C.
Dyer, *Village, Hamlet and Field: Changing Medieval Settlements in Central England*, Windgather Press, 2001.

R. Muir, *The Lost Villages of Britain*, M. Joseph, 1986.

B. Roberts, *The Making of the English Village*, Longman, 1987.

T. Rowley & J. Wood, *Deserted Villages*, Shire Archaeology, 1995.

T. Rowley, *Villages in the Landscape*, Orion, 1994.

Village Studies

L. Bond, *Tyneham: A Lost Heritage*, The Dovecote Press Ltd, 1984.

G. Hannah (ed.), *The Deserted Village: The Diary of an Oxfordshire Rector, James Newton, of Nuneham Courtenay, 1736-86*, Alan Sutton Publishing Ltd, 1992.

R. Legg, *Tyneham*, Dorset Publishing Company, 2002.

S. Melia, *Hallsands, A Village Betrayed*, Forest Publishing, 2002

R. & W. F. Milton, *Sisters Against the Sea: The Remarkable Story of Hallsands*, Devon Books, 2005.

A. Norman & M. Hurst, *Tyneham: The Lost Village of Dorset*, Halsgrove, 2005.

E. & H. Perry, *Tottington: A Lost Village in Norfolk*, George Reeve Ltd, 1999.

R. Sawyer, *Little Imber on the Down: Salisbury Plain's Ghost Village*, Hobnob Press, 2001.

P. Wright, *The Village that died for England: The Strange Story of Tyneham*, Vintage, 1996.

USEFUL ADDRESSES

English Heritage
Customer Services Department
PO Box 569
Swindon
SN2 2YP
email: customers@english-heritage.org.uk
www.english-heritage.org.uk

The National Trust
PO Box 39
Warrington
WA5 7WD
email: enquiries@thenational-trust.org.uk
www.nationaltrust.org.uk

The National Archives
Kew
Richmond
Surrey
TW9 4DU
www.nationalarchives.gov.uk

Web Sites

English Villages
www.eng-villages.co.uk

Medieval Settlement Research Group
www.britarch.ac.uk/msrg

Local County Record offices and the County Council Historic Environment Record (formerly the Sites and Monuments Record) are also useful.

GLOSSARY

Assart
An area of waste – frequently woodland – that was cleared to become agricultural land. The word was also used to describe a piece of newly cultivated or reclaimed land.

Borough (*also* burgh, burh, burg)
In the late 9th and early-10th centuries a 'burh', or 'burg', was a fortified settlement that enjoyed a degree of self-governance and privileges. The later medieval borough was a town or city that had obtained a royal charter confirming similar rights and privileges and a licence to hold markets.

Burgage (plot)
In medieval boroughs, the properties of burgesses, the citizens or freemen (*see below*) of the town, were held by a tenure known as burgage, a form of freehold for which a yearly rent was paid, or trade or manufactured goods were rendered.

Carucate
A measure of land based upon the area that a team of eight oxen could plough in a year. It was dependant upon local soil quality and topography, although it usually averaged about 48 hectares (120 acres). A carucate was commonly used as the unit of assessment for taxation in areas that had once fallen within the Danelaw, and is roughly comparable to the Saxon 'hide' (*see below*).

Chapel/chapelry
A chapel-of-ease (a building used for religious worship) was often built in a remote, outlying part of a large parish, or in a parish so populous that the primary church did not suffice. Some chapels later acquired the right to hold baptisms, marriages and burials, becoming parish churches in their own right in the 19th century. The district served by such a chapel was known as a chapelry.

Close
A small field enclosed by a wall or hedge either at the periphery of a cultivated area, or taken from the open field and removed from the communal farming system.

Common (land)
Land outside the primary area of cultivation, upon which certain members of the community had the right to graze animals, cut turf, collect firewood, catch fish or extract sand, gravel and stone.

Court of Chancery
The High Court of Chancery was one of the earliest courts of equity. Its origins are known to date from the time of King John (1167–1216). It became a court of law during the reign of Edward III (1312–77), when the Chancellor was given the power to hear petitions to the King, and gained jurisdiction over cases that fell outside the remit of Common Law. Many of the cases heard in chancery concerned disputes over land and property.

Crew yard
An open yard where livestock were kept in the winter months.

Croft
An enclosed piece of land attached to a house or cottage. Crofts were often bounded by ditches and banks, upon which hedges might be planted.

Demesne
The land within a manor that was cultivated for the profit of the lord by peasants as part of their work obligations, possibly alongside a group of retained farmworkers known as the 'famuli'.

Domesday Survey/Book
In 1086, William the Conqueror commissioned a survey of the territory he had won 20 years before. By August 1086, the value and ownership of 13,418 English settlements had been recorded, not only in their current condition, but also as they had been before the Norman Conquest. Eventually, the individual returns were written up in two great ledgers known as the Domesday Book. Today the book is at the National Archives in Kew, London.

Enclosure
The subdivision of common land for individual ownership, usually enforced by means of ditches and fences or hedges.

Field walking
An archeological investigation during which an area of land is systematically examined and searched on foot. The distribution of any artefacts and/or archaeological features identified provide clues as to the use of the land over time and can sometimes suggest sites of former habitation.

Freemen/Free tenants (freehold)
A freeman usually, although not always, held freehold property, for which he paid rent. He was often permitted to transfer this property to another, usually through inheritance. A borough freeman was a member of an enfranchised community and possessed the rights granted to that community by its lord.

Furlong

A unit of measurement defined by the length of a furrow ploughed across an open field, most often given as 201m (220 yards). The term also describes the blocks into which individual strips were organized, and which followed a particular crop rotation.

Glebe (land)

Land belonging to the church that was farmed or leased by the parish priest to supplement his income.

Grange (Monastic)

An outlying farm or estate, often acquired by a monastery through gift or bequest and worked by lay brothers or hired labourers. Monastic granges normally included a chapel among the administration and farm buildings.

Hamlet

Along with isolated farmsteads, hamlets are thought to have been ancient forms of agricultural settlement predating the nucleated village, and still prevalent in many areas. There are also examples of hamlets being created by the shrinkage of a nucleated village.

Hide

Like the carucate (*see above*), this was a variable unit of land measurement, usually about 48.5 hectares (120 acres), depending upon the quality of the land. It was also used for tax assessment purposes. The extent was determined by the area that could be annually ploughed by a team of eight oxen, and was deemed sufficient to support a family.

Hollow-way

A sunken lane, often forming the main street of a village, which has been worn beneath the level of the surrounding ground as a result of erosion. Hollow-way depth is sometimes exaggerated by the raised banks and house-platforms that were often ranged along either side.

Infield/Outfield

In villages with large areas of poor soil, the infield/outfield system became the characteristic form of open-field agriculture. The infield consisted of strips of land close to the settlement that were commonly farmed, and were cultivated in rotation to produce the main grain crops. The outfield lay beyond this intensively farmed area, and was frequently left uncultivated, reverting to natural grassland or heath.

Lay Subsidy

Lay subsidies were taxes that were used by the Crown to raise money for specific purposes, for example, military campaigns.

Longhouse

A rectangular building in which a dwelling space and byre or workshop were combined. The two areas were accessed by a common doorway that opened into a roughly central dividing passage.

Manor

A manor was both a territorial unit held by a landlord and an economic unit, usually comprising the demesne (*see above*), the holdings of the tenants and glebe land (*see above*).

Mansae

A mansae, or manse, was a large and imposing house, for example, a mansion.

Messuage

A dwelling house, together with its outbuildings, yard and any surrounding property or 'appurtenances', particularly large examples being referred to as 'capital messuages'.

Motte and bailey castle

The motte was a low circular or oval mound constructed from earth and stone, the top of which was level for use as a lookout point. A wooden bailey (a fortified compound) was sometimes added. The entire complex was surrounded by a defensive rampart and deep ditch that could be crossed by a wooden bridge.

Murrain

An infectious disease in livestock, notably cattle and sheep.

Open-field agriculture

A system of large, unenclosed fields, generally associated with nucleated villages and the intensive cultivation of corn, whereby the agricultural land of the parish was divided into long, thin strips grouped together. The creation and exploitation of these fields was a collective effort by the community, with resources such as oxen and ploughs shared between the holders of the strips.

Parish

An area whose tithes (*see below*) supported the primary local place of worship. Most of England's medieval parishes were in existence by 1200, by which time many were already several centuries old.

Placea

Medieval Latin for a place, or plot of land, often a piece of flat ground.

Ploughland

A unit of tax assessment based on the amount of potential arable land an estate possessed, expressed as an estimate of the number of ploughs that were needed to cultivate it.

Plough team

The pairs of draft animals that pulled medieval ploughs, usually oxen, although horses were sometimes used on lighter soils towards the end of the Middle Ages.

Ridge and furrow (*also* rig and furrow)

The earthwork remains formed by a medieval ploughing technique that was repeated on the same strips for many years to build up significant ridges.

Ringwork

Defensive earthworks dating from the Norman period, ringworks are mounds surrounded by ditches and are the precursors of motte and bailey castles (*see above*).

Serf/Serfdom

A wide-ranging designation of personal status. Serfs were the property of the lord and, as such, could be sold or given away. Their movement was severely restricted, as was their ability to own land or marry freely.

Sokeman

A free villager who was usually able to leave or sell his land at will. As with the freeman (*see above*), a sokeman might owe services or rent, and could be obliged to attend his lord's court.

Solar

Often found in substantial medieval dwellings, a solar was the householder's living room, or private chamber.

Sondage

A fairly deep archaeological test in a limited area made to determine whether more extensive excavation is warranted.

Tithe

The 8th-century custom of giving one tenth of all produce from an area of land to support the parish priest. Tithes became a mandatory tax levied on harvests and animals in AD 855. Originally paid in kind, over the centuries tithes were increasingly commuted to money payments.

Toft

A plot of land upon which a village house stood, along with outbuildings and perhaps a small enclosed yard or garden.

Township

An ancient term for the smallest unit of local government and taxation. It comprised a rural community, with its lands and other resources, and was later known as a 'vill'.

Villein

Although members of the dependant peasantry, villeins were the wealthiest class of serfs or unfree tenants of manorial land under the feudal system.

Waste

Land outside the primary area of cultivation, such as woodland, fenland or heath. In the Domesday Book, 'waste' was used to describe land from which no tax was forthcoming.

Yeoman

Originally applied to the servants of a knight, by Tudor times 'yeoman' was commonly used to refer to prosperous farmers and sometimes tradesmen. They were below the rank of the gentry, but above that of the husbandman.

INDEX

Picture Credits

All pictures are by Stephen Whitehorne, except as follows:

Pages: 10, 119(b) Luttrell Psalter, Windmill image Add.42130 f158, by permission of the British Library; 46(b): Sheep image Add.42130 f23v, by permission of the British Library; 12: courtesy of Weald Downland Open Air Museum, Singleton, West Sussex; 24, 46(t), 48, 83(b), 92(b), 96(t) 121(t), 116(t), 132(b), 154(t), 162(b): copyright reserved Cambridge University Collection of Air Photographs (ULM); 34(t) : courtesy of Steve Hartgroves, Historic Environment Service, Cornwall County Council; 43(b), 44: by kind permission of the Wiltshire Archaeological Society Library; 45: The National Archives, ref. WO 32/17163; 53: reproduced with the kind permission of the Ordnance Survey; 60, 74 (b), 102(t): courtesy of Cambridge University Collection of Air Photographs, Unit for Landscape Modelling; 74 (t), 76(t), 77: courtesy of Bedfordshire County Council; 80(b): The National Archives, ref.: C1/1009/39; 86(b): © Norfolk Museums & Archaeology Service, photo by Derek A Edwards; 98(b): The National Archives, ref.: C 143/268/28; 109(t): The National Archives, ref.: IR/30/14/116; 112(b): The National Archives, ref.: C1/1348/52; 123(b): The National Archives, ref.: E179/382/13/6; 125: courtesy of the Record Office for Leicestershire Leicester & Rutland; 134(t,b): reproduced with the kind permission of Old Hall, Tatton Park, Cheshire; 138, 140(t): Burdett's 1791 map courtesy of the Derbyshire Records Office; 150: The National Archives, ref.: ED/2/488; 160: The National Archives, ref.:MR/1/1969/3; 164(t):The National Archives, ref.: IR/30/25/467.

Acknowledgements

This book could not have been written without the generous assistance of the following people:

Rose Desmond Air Photo Library Unit for Landscape Modelling, University of Cambridge; Liz Gawith, Enquiry & Research Services - Archaeology & Aerial Photography, English Heritage; Bruce Howard, Archaeology & Historic Buildings Environment Department, Hampshire County Council; Weald & Downland Open Air Museum; Dr Bill Bevan, Survey/Conservation Archaeologist, Cultural Heritage Team, Peak District National Park Authority; Professor Christopher Dyer, Bob Davey, Bronwyn Denny, Christine Wilkinson, John Darlington, Matt Tompkins, Steffanie Brown, Sarah Larter, Charlotte Judet, Sheila Sleath, Jeremy Bourne, Colonel Kiddie (Stanford Battle Training Area), Malcolm Street, Jeremy Wilton (The Four Shires), Bob Baxter (Yorkshire Water), Mary Barley and Brian Ives (Nidderdale Museum), Jan Allen (Norfolk Archaeology), Colin Pendleton (Suffolk Archaeology), Lorna Thornton (Cornhills, Kirkwhelpington), Dr M Nevell, Rob Edwards (Cheshire County Council), Tim Grubb (Gloucestershire County Council Archaeology Service), Lee White (Durham County Council), Deborah Overton, Penny Ward (Shropshire County Council), Julia Wise (Buckinghamshire County Council), Emma Jones (Warwickshire Sites and Monuments Record), Steve Hartgroves (Cornwall County Council), Stephen R. Coleman (Bedfordshire County Council) and all SMR and HER officers throughout England. Special thanks must go to my family for their unfailing patience and support.